RULES TO SPEAK BY

Praise for *Rules to Speak By*

Rules to Speak By delivers practical, easy-to-apply techniques that can immediately level-up your public speaking. I highly recommend it to any attorney committed to reaching their full potential.

Elizabeth Carroll
Director of Legal Writing and Advocacy Program
USC Gould School of Law

Snow is a great source of knowledge and wisdom about how to effectively communicate and conduct trials. His tips are extremely valuable for lawyers of all levels.

Jeff Chemerinsky
Partner
Kendall Brill & Kelly LLP

This is an easy read full of insights on one of the most important—and challenging—professional skills. Our ability to effectively connect with a live audience will only become more critical as technology reshapes our writing process and written work product. This accessible book helps public speakers understand what works, what doesn't, and why, so they can deliver remarks like the best orators. All law students and legal professionals would benefit from reviewing the proven strategies Snow distills and illustrates in this delightful and valuable book. It will benefit anyone who seeks to grab and hold the attention of colleagues, students, or decision makers.

Rebekah Hanley
LRW Clinical Professor
University of Oregon School of Law

RULES TO SPEAK BY

Present and Persuade like the Country's Best Lawyers

John G. Snow

CAROLINA ACADEMIC PRESS
Durham, North Carolina

Library of Congress Cataloging-in-Publication Data

Names: Snow, John G. author
Title: Rules to speak by : present and persuade like the country's best lawyers / John G. Snow.
Description: Durham : Carolina Academic Press, 2026. | Includes bibliographical references and index.
Identifiers: LCCN 2026008182 | ISBN 9781531034863 paperback | ISBN 9781531034870 ebook
Subjects: LCSH: Lawyers--Language | Trial practice--United States | Trial practice | Persuasion (Rhetoric)
Classification: LCC KF8915 .S655 2026
LC record available at https://lccn.loc.gov/2026008182

Carolina Academic Press
700 Kent Street
Durham, North Carolina 27701
(919) 489-7486
www.cap-press.com

Printed in the United States of America

To Chelsea, Rocco, Mom, and Dad

Contents

Preface

You bought a book, not a preface. And the title says it all. This is a book of public speaking lessons for lawyers. In other words, how to talk to juries, judges, colleagues, and clients.

The lessons are built around ten rules. The rules are designed to help the audience. If we follow them, our speeches will be better, the audience will pay more attention, and we will be more persuasive. Please turn to Chapter 1 and jump in.

If you must learn more about me or the origin of this book before starting, you can go to the end where I've included that information. That's also where I've said nice things about my family and friends. Feel free to go there, but come back.

THE TEN RULES OF PUBLIC SPEAKING

1

Rule One: Don't Be Boring

- 1.1 Grab Their Attention Immediately
- 1.2 Fuel the Fire with Knowledge Gaps
- 1.3 Bring Movement and Change to the Room

Don't be boring. This is as good a place to start as any. Plus, it has science on its side.

In the book *Brain Rules*, brain scientist Dr. John Medina teaches us that "the brain doesn't pay attention to boring things."

This means that before we can impact anyone, we need to get and hold their attention. If we can't, there's no point in talking.

Many people don't appreciate how hard this is. They squander their audience's attention in the first few minutes.

But commanding attention is the doorway to influencing others with our ideas. And isn't that the goal?

To be a great public speaker, we should treat our audience the way big-wave surfers treat the ocean—with awe and respect. Legendary surfer Greg Noll put it like this: "If you don't understand the wave, you can't respect it. And if you don't have respect, it's only a matter of time before the ocean teaches you to get some."

Don't take anything for granted. When we speak, we are asking people to give us their most valuable resource—their attention—with the chance to change how they see the world. It is an awesome task. It should be approached accordingly.

We can't assume interest is there just because they came to see us. We need to earn it every minute.

Being able to influence another person with our words is a form of power—and it is available to anyone if they work at it. The other two forms of power—strength and money—are not. To have influence, practice speaking.

The problem lawyers face is that most of us are not taught speaking skills. Instead, we are shown how to be boring. Many law school classes are boring, especially when professors put more energy into their research papers than their lectures.

Law school also prioritizes writing skills over speaking skills. Now, writing skills are important for lawyers—especially with judges eliminating oral arguments.[1] But the problem is that lawyers assume their strong writing skills will translate to a good speech. As you will see in Chapter 5, they won't. In some cases, they'll get in our way.

The other issue is lawyers like to play it safe by imitating each other. So we repeat the bad examples we see. This is why our speeches start the same way. We thank the audience for being there. We introduce ourselves, even if someone else already has (aka the "double intro"). We talk about our credentials, give them an agenda for the day, and say we hope they will find it interesting. We apologize for not being as prepared as we'd like or for it being long.

None of this helps.

We do the same thing when we talk to juries. We introduce ourselves every time we stand up. We thank them whenever we get the chance. We tell them what a privilege it is to represent our client. We tell them how much we respect their time and attention. We explain the reason for what we're doing before we do it—even when the judge already has (aka the "double explanation"). We apologize for taking their time.

Here is an example from the beginning of the prosecution's closing argument in the criminal trial against Conrad Murray, the doctor charged with killing Michael Jackson:

> Good morning, everyone. Let me begin by—and I think I extend this from all the parties and everyone involved in this trial—uh, just first thank each and every one of you, uh, for your service, in this case, uh, for being an extremely, uh, by all accounts punctual, diligent, and attentive jury. Uh, all the parties appreciate it and, uh, all the parties would ask that you hang on a bit longer, uh, while we get through this last phase of the trial. As the court indicated, this is a closing argument and it gives us an opportunity to go through the evidence that you've heard to, uh, ap-

1. *See* Mark A. Neubauer, *The Disappearing Oral Argument*, Litigation, Winter 2022.

> ply that evidence to the law and to present the case in a final summation. Uh, you've heard from I believe 49 witnesses, uh, you've been, uh, presented with 330 plus, uh, exhibits throughout the case extending weeks, um, multiple items of evidence to consider. At the end of the day, however, and as I spoke to you about during voir dire, this case will come down to whether or not you believe Conrad Murray acted with gross negligence or criminal negligence in his treatment of Michael Jackson.

That is what the prosecutor said in the first minute of his closing argument, when the jury's attention was at its highest.

Let's break down what it included:

1. A long-winded thank you (51 words)
2. Asking them to **"hang on a bit longer ... while we get through this"** (this might be the biggest public speaking crime)
3. Repeating information the judge just told them about closing argument
4. Reminding them how long the trial had been and how much evidence they already sat through

If you were on the jury, would this make you excited for what's next? Would this make you want to pay attention?

Unfortunately, this is how many closing arguments start. Keep in mind, this is a *good* lawyer trying one of the most high-profile cases of the year. This type of intro is so common that it is hard to fault him for it. The reason attorneys start this way is they've seen others do it. That, itself, is a problem because interest is created by unexpectedness, by being original.

If people think they know what we're about to say, they won't listen when we say it. They'll be thinking of something more interesting, like what's for dinner.

1.1 Grab Their Attention Immediately

When I teach public speaking to lawyers, I don't start the way most CLE seminars do. I don't thank the audience for being there. I don't introduce myself or go over my credentials. I don't give them an agenda for the day. And I don't discuss "housekeeping" items.

Instead, I drop a mysterious bag on the table, pull out a Super Soaker, pump it three times, and ask, "Who's ready to learn about public speaking?"

Then I pause. I tell them to look around. I ask them to notice if anyone is looking at their phones. The answer is no. They're all engaged.

I ask them to tell me the last time they were in a lecture where the room looked like this. Most can't remember.

I put the water gun down and explain what I did—I grabbed their attention by breaking their expectations for how a talk should start. I made everyone curious about what was coming next.

"Are we going to get wet?" "What does this water gun have to do with public speaking?" "Is this guy insane?"

No matter what question they were asking, they all decided I was worth paying attention to.

We talk about "grabbing" attention for a reason. Merriam-Webster's Dictionary defines "grab" as "to take or seize by or as if by a sudden motion or grasp," "to take hastily," or "a sudden snatch."

This shows the logic in the phrase "grab attention." The phrase understands that we need to act swiftly and suddenly to get attention. We can't request it politely; we need to grab it.

I could grab attention in less-gimmicky ways when I teach this. I could say something provocative. I could ask an unexpected question. Both are great tools.

But I choose the Super Soaker because it is a memorable gimmick, and I can connect it to my point—that they should start every talk with a "Super-Soaker moment."

This does not mean bring a water gun to every talk you give. The water gun works for my public-speaking talk only because it illustrates the specific point I want to make about public speaking—that it is important to start our talks in a sudden, surprising, and intriguing way.

Our "grabber" needs to relate to our message in a meaningful way. If not, it will be like annoying clickbait on the internet—it will grab our audience's attention, but they'll be disappointed when the information offered next doesn't live up to the hook. Anyone would be disappointed if they clicked on an article titled "Three Secrets to Transform Your Life," only to find advice that isn't secret at all—"eat healthy," "get sleep," and "exercise."

I'm not the first lawyer to understand the importance of grabbing attention suddenly. While they don't call them "Super-Soaker moments," skilled trial lawyers have used "grabbers" for years. They don't start like the Conrad Murray closing.

Let's look at some examples.

EXAMPLE 1: OKLAHOMA CITY BOMBING TRIAL

In this trial, Timothy McVeigh was prosecuted for the deadliest act of domestic terrorism in United States history. The case had great national importance. Here is how prosecutor Joseph Hartzler started his opening:

> April 19th, 1995, was a beautiful day in Oklahoma City—at least it started out as a beautiful day.[2]

Notice what he achieves in one sentence. He jumps in, sets the scene, and creates suspense. The jury immediately wants to know how the day shifted. How it became no longer beautiful.

EXAMPLE 2: AMBER GUYGER TRIAL

This case also made headlines. The defendant was an off-duty police officer who was prosecuted for fatally shooting an unarmed accountant in his own apartment. She claimed that she believed (wrongly) that the man was a burglar in her own apartment, which was also in the building. The case raised racial bias issues because the defendant was white, and the victim was black.

How did prosecutor Jason Fine start his closing argument?

With a grabber. You can watch it online.[3]

After ten seconds of dramatic silence, he picked up a piece of paper and read a quote from the defendant's testimony: "I never want anybody to ever have to go through or even imagine going through what I felt that night."

He noted this was one of the last things the defendant said on the stand. Then he asked out loud, "Are you kidding me?"

He crumpled up the paper and threw it in a trashcan, saying "that is garbage, most of what she said was garbage."

Just like the first example, this is sudden, unexpected, and instantly provokes questions. The prosecutor is challenging the defendant's testimony and has the jury wondering, "What is he going to expose?" "Were we lied to?" "What did we miss?"

---

2. *United States v. Timothy McVeigh* (Oklahoma City Bombing Trial), opening statement, April 24, 1997, available at https://www.famous-trials.com/oklacity/727-hartzleropening.

3. *Texas v. Amber Guyger*, closing argument, Sept. 30, 2019, available at https://www.youtube.com/watch?v=5fdEGjYsS7I.

EXAMPLE 3: FLORIDA V. BRENTON BUTLER

This criminal trial was the subject of the 2001 Academy-Award winning documentary, *Murder on a Sunday Morning*. In it, a 15-year-old black boy was wrongfully accused of murdering a middle-aged white tourist outside a motel in Jacksonville, Florida. He was ultimately acquitted, and the real killer was found shortly after.

The defense strategy was to attack the sloppy police work that led to the boy's arrest.

Here's how defense attorney Patrick McGuinness started his closing:

> Winston Churchill used to say that "the quality of a nation's civilization can be measured by the methods its police use in the enforcement of its criminal laws." I suggest to you that by that yard stick, we're in deep trouble....

Again, it's sudden, unexpected, intriguing. He's connected the case to a timeless quote and has the jury wondering about how they are all in "deep trouble."

EXAMPLE 4: THE ENRON TRIAL

This was the prosecution of Enron's two main executives for one of the biggest accounting scandals in U.S. History.

Here's how prosecutor John Hueston began his opening statement:

> Ladies and gentlemen, the United States in this case will take you inside the doors of what was the seventh largest corporation in this country: Enron.[4]

Then he projected a picture of the Enron tower, while stating:

> Let me bring you to a critical turning point in the story that you will hear about at trial. Mid-August of 2001. To the outside world, Enron appeared to be a picture of corporate success: 28,000 employees and growing, named the world's most innovative company year after year, a seemingly magical ability to make earnings of 15 to 20 percent growth year after year. But inside the doors of Enron, something was terribly wrong.

4. *United States v. Jeffrey Skilling* (Enron prosecution), opening statement, Jan. 31, 2006.

Hueston later explained that he purposefully crafted his opening to create "a sense of excitement in the jury; a way to entice them to join us on a journey through the evidence, into a world normally foreclosed to them."[5] Ultimately, he wanted to convey a "sense of mystery and dram."

Notice what these examples and my silly water-gun stunt share—a sense of mystery and drama.

Notice also what they don't do. They don't start with "thank yous." They don't start with credentials. They don't start with agendas.

None of them needs these things.

These attorneys show they appreciate the jury by engaging them and not wasting their time—not by saying thank you. They show their expertise through their content—not by talking about themselves. And because they've hooked their audience, they don't need agendas for people to follow along.

Outside the legal world, presentation experts agree that the grabber is the best way to start. In *Pitch Perfect: How to Say It Right the First Time, Every Time*, professional media coach Bill McGowan writes:

> The first thirty seconds of any conversation or presentation are like the last two minutes of a football game. This is when victory or defeat is determined, the period of time when your audience is deciding whether you are interesting enough for them to continue paying attention. Say just the right thing, and the communication game is yours.... Get it wrong, and your listeners start daydreaming, checking their smartphones, or plotting their conversation exit strategy.[6]

He recommends that every opening have three characteristics—it should be short, suspenseful, and surprising. Just like the examples we looked at.

In their guide "Making Your Presentation Stick," *New York Times* bestselling authors Chip and Dan Heath write:

> The first mission of a presentation is to grab attention. And that's why it's disturbing that many presentations stumble out of the gate with a preamble—a laborious overview of what's going to be covered.[7]

---

5. John C. Hueston, *Behind the Scenes of the Enron Trial: Creating the Decisive Moments*, 44 Am. Crim. L. Rev. 197 (2007).

6. Bill McGowan, Pitch Perfect: How to Say It Right the First Time, Every Time 48 (2016).

7. *Making Your Presentation Stick* (October 20, 2008), *madetostick.com/blog*.

Instead, they recommend you "[t]oss out the preamble and parachute into the action."

Follow this advice with your next presentation—whether to a jury at trial or colleagues at a CLE. Nail the first 30 seconds. Convince your audience you are worth paying attention to. Do or say something a little unexpected, dramatic, and mysterious. If you lose your audience at the beginning, you may never get them back.

Caveats for Talking to Judges and Partners

This advice needs to be tweaked for two audiences—judges and law firm partners. They don't want mystery and drama. They are busy and want to quickly know if you have the answer they're looking for. If you don't show them you do, they'll get frustrated and stop paying attention. Thus, you still have a small window to convince them you're worth paying attention to, but how you do it is different.

The difference between judges and partners, on the one hand, and juries and CLE audiences, on the other, is that judges and partners are already interested in what you have to say, but it's a very specific type of interest focused on solving a problem. Juries and CLE audiences are more interested in being entertained. That's not to say judges and partners aren't too, but it's not their main interest.

So with judges and partners, jump right to the issue and your proposed resolution. Tone down the drama, skip the mystery, and don't meander. That's how you grab their attention.

This is what the best appellate advocates do. Take the following example from Supreme Court litigator Lisa Blatt, arguing a trademark infringement case for whiskey-maker Jack Daniels. At the time, she had the highest Supreme Court win rate of any attorney in private practice.

> Mr. Chief Justice, and may it please the Court: This case involves a dog toy that copies Jack Daniel's trademark and trade dress and associates its whiskey with dog poop. After a four-day trial, the district court found both infringement

> and dilution. The Ninth Circuit erroneously reversed both rulings.[8]

She doesn't thank the court. She doesn't say how happy she is to be there. She doesn't mention that she knows the court has already read the briefs. She parachutes in. It's safe to say she had their attention.

Blatt also honors the rituals of the venue, which is important. In the Supreme Court, it is customary to start just as Blatt did: "Mr. Chief Justice, and may it please the Court."[9] Begin this way if you ever present there.

Edward L. Lascher, a great appellate lawyer, once said, "It is a pleasingly brief and ritualistic touch to open with 'May it please the Court'; it is a crashingly boring waste of time to describe sycophantically how happy counsel is to be there."[10]

The same applies when a busy law firm partner calls you to their office for your thoughts on a case. Start with your recommendation about how to handle the case, and then back it up.

The best formula is to give your recommendation followed by your top two or three reasons. For example:

- "We should skip a motion to dismiss and try to beat this case at summary judgment, for three reasons. **First**, the plaintiff's allegations are strong enough to overcome a motion to dismiss, so it will waste our client's time and money, and could lose credibility with the court. **Second**, it seems unlikely the plaintiff can develop evidence to support the second element of their claim and caselaw in our state supports trial courts granting summary judgment on this issue. **Third**, building a record for our motion won't require much discovery, so we can still file it early in the litigation."

Here are some wrong ways to answer a law firm partner's question (in person or in email):

- **"That's a great question and something I spent a lot of time thinking about"**—This gets you nothing with the partner. Instead, it signals that you haven't thought enough about it and are buying

---

8. *Jack Daniel's Properties, Inc. v. VIP Products LLC.*, No. 22-148, Oral Argument, March 22, 2023.

9. ANTONIN SCALIA & BRYAN A. GARNER, MAKING YOUR CASE: THE ART OF PERSUADING JUDGES 166 (2008).

10. *Id.*

time to think of an answer. The partner will lose confidence in you and once they lose confidence, they'll stop listening. If you need a moment to compose yourself before speaking, just pause (more on this in Chapter 7.2).

- **"First let me tell you how I researched this. I started by looking at ..."**—Don't start describing your process. Start with your result because that is what they want. If they want to know how you got there, they will ask. But first give them what they want, and then back it up with reasons.
- **"Well this is a tricky issue and there's not a lot of authority directly on point for it"**—Most questions lawyers deal with are tricky, and unprecedented issues are common. If your issue falls into one of these categories, the partner probably already knows it. Starting this way only delays telling them what they want to know and signals you aren't confident in your recommendation. Instead, start with your recommendation and then explain why you recommend it despite a lack of authority. Done this way, they will appreciate your problem-solving skills in a grey area.
- **"It's hard to predict what a court will do here, but ..."**—Like the last example, starting with a hedge like this might state the obvious. It also delays the information the partner wants and signals a lack of confidence.
- **"In researching this I was surprised (or frustrated) to find ..."**—The partner isn't interested in your internal reaction to the question. Instead, they want to know what your recommendation is. So keep your surprise or frustration to yourself.
- **"Okay, so bear with me ..."**—Never start any speech like this. All it says is that you have not thought enough about how to present your information clearly and succinctly.

Office culture created the phrase "too long; didn't read" for emails that are too long and bury their main point. We should consider a similar phrase for speaking—"too long; didn't listen." If we waste our audience's time and take too long to say something interesting, they'll tune out. So unless our speaking event requires us to speak for a set amount of time—like CLE lectures that have minimum time requirements—we should keep our speeches short and to the point.

1.2 Fuel the Fire with Knowledge Gaps

Once we have our audience's attention, the next challenge is keeping it.

A basic truth about attention is that it wanes over time until it dies. Researchers can't agree on how long we have,[11] but if we don't do anything to keep the audience's attention, it will eventually drop off like we see in Figure 1.

Figure 1: Audience Attention Over Time

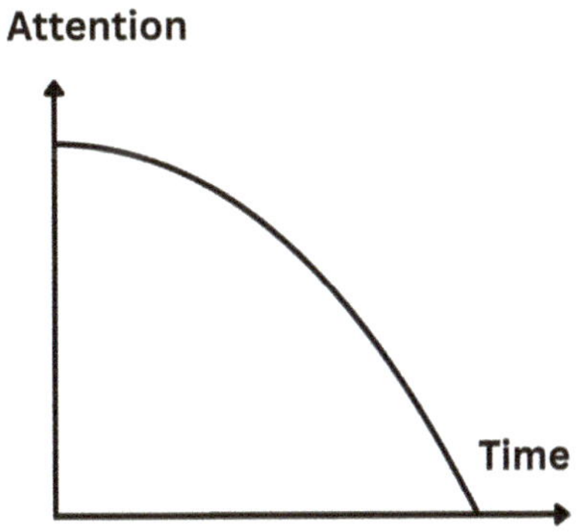

Yet if we work hard to keep the audience's attention throughout, it can look like Figure 2.

Figure 2: Audience Attention Over Time (With Hard Work)

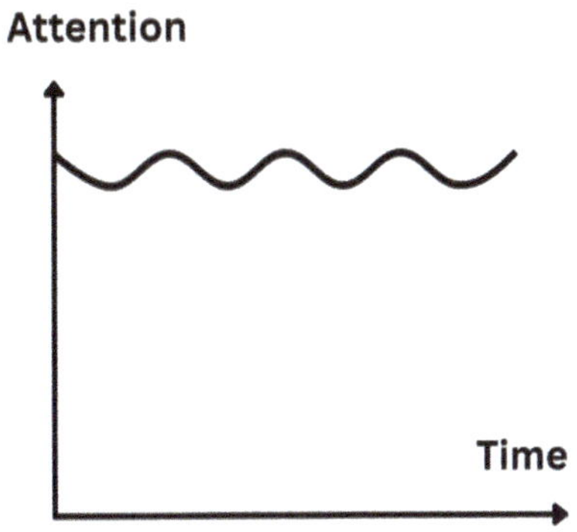

11. Many swear by a 10–15-minute rule—also popularized by the TED Talk organization—but others claim there are wide individual differences and that it depends on the content. *See* Karen Wilson & James H. Korn, *Attention During Lectures: Beyond Ten Minutes*, 34 Teaching of Psychol. 85 (Fall 2007).; Neil A. Bradbury, *Attention Span During Lectures: 8 Seconds, 10 Minutes, or More?*, 40 Advances in Physiology Educ. 509 (2016).

In Figure 2, each upward swing represents something the speaker did to reignite the audience's curiosity.

The best analogy for attention during a talk is a campfire. We need a spark to light it. Then if we don't do anything to keep it going, it will die, and we don't know exactly when. But if we add fuel, we can keep it alive.

Bill McGowan—author of *Pitch Perfect*—learned this writing for TV. He learned to write scripts that "relentlessly held attention" with "an attention-grabbing opening followed by another attention-grabbing line roughly every twenty to thirty seconds."[12]

Brain scientist John Medina learned this giving lectures. After struggling to maintain attention, he started breaking 50-minute classes into 10-minute modules. When each one ended, he introduced a new hook.[13] He writes:

> When I started placing hooks in my lectures, I immediately noticed changes in the audience members' attitudes. First, they were still interested at the end of the first 10 minutes. Second, they seemed able to maintain their attention for another 10 minutes or so, as long as another hook was supplied at the end. I could win the battle for their attention in 10-minute increments.[14]

So how do we add fuel to the fire and keep attention? How do we design good hooks?

Here are three ways:

1. Posing a new question or sub-question,
2. Introducing a new twist in a story, or
3. Sharing a surprising bit of new information that is relevant to the audience.

All three tools work for the same reason—they expose a new "knowledge gap." That means they highlight something the audience doesn't know and create a burning desire for them to know more about it. Exposing knowledge gaps works especially well after we've already shown the audience that we know how to give them valuable information. It's like we've become their favorite restaurant, and they want to come back for more.

---

12. McGowan, cited above in note 6, at 58.
13. John Medina, Brain Rules 89–92 (2008).
14. *Id.* at 92.

This is explained by the "gap theory" of curiosity. The theory was created in the 1990s by a behavioral economist at Carnegie Mellon named George Loewenstein (he's also Sigmund Freud's grandson). Lowenstein argues that curiosity arises when we feel a gap "between what we know and what we want to know."[15] This gap "feels like a mental itch, a mosquito bite on the brain."[16] We stay tuned because that's how we relieve the pain.

Consider most of the things that hold our attention—they use knowledge gaps. For example, stories make us wonder what will happen next and how it will all resolve. They are built around knowledge gaps created by introducing a conflict and leaving us in suspense about how it will end. We struggle to put down even bad books when we can't stand not knowing how they finish.

Some of the most successful TV shows and movies are mysteries—"whodunits" and "howcatchems"—where we need to know who committed the crime or how they got caught. Other bingeable shows use knowledge gaps too. They open and close knowledge gaps during an episode, and then right before they finish, they introduce a new twist—a cliffhanger—that forces us to watch the next episode.

Jeopardy!—one of the most successful shows of all time—revolves around knowledge gaps. We have the questions during the show, which each introduce a knowledge gap. Then we have the overarching knowledge gap of "who is going to win?"

Sports games and reality competitions involve knowledge gaps—"Who will win?" And if we bet on them, "Were we right?"

These knowledge gaps make us uncomfortable, and we enjoy when they are resolved. It's a form of tension and release.

The release is a critical component. When we use knowledge gaps, we can't leave the audience hanging for too long because they will get frustrated with us. Thus, we not only have to create the knowledge gap, but we also need to show that we have the answer. If not, they'll start looking for it elsewhere (like their phone).

In the end, holding attention often boils down to opening knowledge gaps and then filling them. The Heath brothers recommend this in their book *Made*

15. Jonah Lehrer, *The Itch of Curiosity*, WIRED Science (Aug 3, 2010), https://www.wired.com/2010/08/the-itch-of-curiosity/ (quoting George Lowenstein); *see also* George Lowenstein, *The Psychology of Curiosity: A Review and Reinterpretation*, 116 Psychol. Bull. 75 (1994).

16. *Id.*

to Stick: "We can engage people's curiosity over a long period of time by systematically 'opening gaps' in their knowledge—and then filling those gaps."[17]

So good talks typically follow this format:

1. "Hey, here is a really profound question or idea I bet you've never thought about but probably should."
2. "Let's solve it together. I'll be your guide. I have the answer. Here is how I got there."
3. "OK, wow, we all learned something from that. To sum it up, here's what I've said. But now that we've learned this, it takes us to this other interesting question. I bet you've never thought about this either. OK, let's solve it together."

When we're done opening and filling relevant knowledge gaps, sum it up and sit down.

* * *

Many lawyers don't use this tool. Instead, we destroy curiosity by giving away everything we are going to say in a detailed "overview" or "roadmap" at the beginning.

This has two problems. First, we've jumped to feeding the audience information without sparking curiosity in it. Second, ideas are most interesting the first time the audience hears them. If we give our audience too much in the roadmap, they won't pay attention the second time we say anything because they will think they already know it. We've become predictable, and predictable is boring.

A predictable closing argument starts with a road map like this:

> Good morning, members of the jury. Let me first tell you what I'm going to be talking about in my closing argument. First, I'm going to tell you about the law and the instructions that govern this case. Some of those instructions are __________. Second, I'm going to go over the facts. I'm going to talk about ________, __________, and __________. And third, I'm going to combine the law and the facts to show you what verdict you should reach. Finally, I'm going to talk about some of the things you shouldn't consider. OK, here's the law …

---

17. Chip Heath & Dan Heath, Made to Stick: Why Some Ideas Survive and Others Die 16 (2007).

Now, here is an example of a closing that covers the same material but uses knowledge gaps instead of a road map:

1. **Step One: Introduce the Problem**

   "Members of the jury, this case is going to be yours soon. And you have a very important job. Do you know what that job is? [KNOWLEDGE GAP] Do you know what your verdict will mean in this case? Let me tell you...."

2. **Step Two: Tease the Solution**

   "OK, we've talked about what your verdict means. Do you know the rules for how to get to that verdict? How to do your job? [KNOWLEDGE GAP]

   Most of you have never done this. Did you understand those jury instructions the judge read? What if I broke them down for you in simple terms? What if I told you what will make your job easy when you deliberate? Would that be helpful? [KNOWLEDGE GAP]

   OK, here are the most important instructions in this case...."

3. **Step Three: Throw in a New Wrinkle**

   "OK, now you know what the most important instructions are. That should help you. But you also heard weeks of testimony. Would it also help if I told you what you should focus on? [KNOWLEDGE GAP]

   Three pieces of evidence matter more than anything else you heard. Do you know what they are? [KNOWLEDGE GAP] Here, let me tell you...."

4. **Step Four: Throw in Another Wrinkle**

   "Now you know the rules and the most important evidence. Do you know how to put it together? [KNOWLEDGE GAP] Here, let me show you...."

5. **Step Five: Tell Them What to Watch Out For**

   "Now you know how to do your job. But some juries hear these things and still have trouble. They get hung up considering things they aren't supposed to. And that means it takes them a lot longer to reach their verdict. Do you want to know how to make sure that doesn't happen when you deliberate? [KNOWLEDGE GAP] Here are all the things you shouldn't focus on to reach your verdict...."

6. **Step Six: Tell Them What to Remember, If Nothing Else**
   "OK, we've covered a lot. Now, if you don't remember anything else I told you, there is one thing I absolutely want you to remember when you go back in the jury room. Just one thing. Do you want to know what it is? [KNOWLEDGE GAP] OK, here it is ..."

We can use this same format for a CLE or oral argument. The format doesn't require that we always ask explicit questions like in the example. And it doesn't need to be used rigidly throughout an entire talk. The point is that we should strive to begin each new section of a talk by exposing or reigniting a knowledge gap.

This also doesn't mean our talk should have no discernible structure. It needs a good structure. Studies have shown that clear structures help audiences and learners understand. But whenever we preview our structure to the audience, we need to do it quickly and not give everything away at the expense of destroying curiosity.

Jonah Berger, a marketing professor at the Wharton School of Business, says "sometimes it's better to be uncertain ... because it helps hold attention."[18] In his research, he reviewed a vast amount of online content to see what worked best at holding attention. One of the biggest drivers was uncertainty. It encouraged people to stay tuned. He says that "if we want people to keep consuming a number of ideas to get to the big punch line, we can't give away that big punch line right away."[19]

In the end, have a plan for pulling the audience back in throughout your talk. If I can get more people to do this—and make some presentations less boring—I'll be proud of what I've contributed to the world.

---

18. Interview with Jonah Berger, in *This Advice Will Make You More Persuasive*, Nudge Podcast (Jan. 8, 2024).

19. *Catching Eyes in the Attention Economy*, Wharton Mag. (Spring/Summer 2024), https://magazine.wharton.upenn.edu/issues/spring-summer-2024/catching-eyes-in-the-attention-economy/; Jonah A. Berger, Wendy W. Moe & David A. Schweidel, *What Holds Attention? Linguistic Drivers of Engagement* (unpublished working paper, Dec. 23, 2022), available at https://papers.ssrn.com/sol3/papers.cfm?abstract_id=4311202.

1.3 Bring Movement and Change to the Room

Our third challenge in the fight against boredom is that we talk in boring environments—courtrooms and conference rooms. Unless we bring energy to them, they become monotonous.

In a courtroom, the staff is used to following the same procedures every day. They are bored by it all. The bailiff has said "please rise" so many times that they have no enthusiasm left in their voice.

The next time you are in one of these environments, pay attention to what happens when someone walks in or out of the door. All the heads turn to see who it is, just because that is the most interesting thing in the courtroom at that moment.

Lawyer and advocacy trainer Steven P. Wood observed this on a podcast for the National Institute of Trial Advocacy.[20] He theorized that because courtrooms are such "constant environments," people will pay attention to any change or new thing because it will be the most interesting thing at that time.

I agree.

But we can use this to our advantage by being the ones who introduce the change. Wood says, "What we need to do is introduce change into the courtroom environment to subtly increase the trier of fact's attentiveness."

This doesn't need to be anything drastic. In a boring environment, even small things can make a presentation more interesting. Remember, our competition is the back door—and it doesn't take much to be more interesting than it. If the court lets you move around, leave the lectern and change your position every few minutes, or whenever you discuss a new topic. Change the rhythm and pace of your voice. Speed up; slow down. Vary your gestures.

Transition between different visuals and demonstratives. Fill your slides with pictures and short videos for them to consume. If you have a piece of physical evidence, pull it out half-way through your presentation to give them something new to look at.

These changes, while small, are often enough to keep the audience focused on us.

---

20. *May the Record Reflect Podcast*, Top 10 Trial Tips that Make a Difference, with Steve Wood (Mar. 8, 2021), https://www.nita.org/s/product/21-top-10-tips-that-make-a-difference-with-steve-wood/01t4W00000DaBoPQAV.

In the battle against boredom, we need to bring every weapon we have. Some of these aspects of speaking will be elaborated on in later chapters—*see* Chapter 6 (visuals), Chapter 7 (voice), Chapter 8 (body language). For now, just remember that it takes a plan and effort to not be boring.

2

Rule Two: It's Not About You; It's About Them

It's not about you; it's about them. This works well as our second rule because it also helps us with the first rule. It helps us not be boring. This is because people are most interested in themselves—not us or our clients. If we make our presentations about them and their needs, they will pay attention. If we don't, they will think about something more meaningful to them.

It doesn't stop there. To influence people with our presentations, we also need to think about who they are and how they see the world. Behavioral science tells us people resist ideas that conflict with their preexisting beliefs—no matter how strong the logic is. Thus, if we want our messages to stick, we need to frame them to fit with their beliefs. We need to appeal to the audience in front of us, not some hypothetical one.

Third, we need to recognize something about all people. They don't like being told how to think. They prefer their own ideas. When we present, we need a "show, not tell" approach. We need to help our audience reach our conclusions on their own.

This chapter is about these things.

2.1 Remember Why They're There

Educational psychologists discovered that people pay the most attention to things that are relevant and important to them.[1] Psychologists also discovered that people are bad at spotting information that might be valuable to them. They need to be shown—explicitly—how and why information will help them in their lives.

Professional speakers figured this out too. Scott Berkun, author of *Confessions of a Public Speaker*, gives this advice:

> most of the time when you are bored, it means the person who's speaking ... did not think carefully enough—or possibly not even at all about why you're here.... If you talk about stuff people really care about, they will pay attention.[2]

As presenters who care about holding attention, we should jump on this idea. It begins with thinking about our audience, why they're there, and what they want.

Let's start with the jury.

They are there because they got a summons that forced them to be there. And because they are forced to be there, most jurors want only two things: to get home and to feel good about what they did. It's usually in that order.

Now let's think about judges.

They are there because it's their job. It's how they put a roof over their heads and food on their table. And because it's their job, they also want two things: help doing their job, so they can get home, and to feel good about what they did. Usually in that order.

Now clients.

They come to us because they need to solve a problem. Thus, they want two things: to solve that problem, so they can get home, and to feel good about how they did it.

Now our colleagues.

They come to legal presentations to grow their knowledge and skills—not with random information, but concrete tips they can incorporate into their practice. Thus, they want two things: to get the information, so they can get home, and to feel good about the work they do.

---

1. Susan A. Ambrose et al., How Learning Works 83–84 (2010).

2. Scott Berkun, Confessions of a Public Speaker, Talks at Google (Dec. 15, 2009), https://www.youtube.com/watch?v=yhA04D_xfp8.

You get the point. We usually have two things to offer an audience: help performing a job or task and the chance to feel good. It's the same every time. Every audience wants to eventually get back to their life and feel like they got value from us.

If our information doesn't serve one of these two goals, cut it. If we don't, the audience will punish us for wasting their time. The jury will vote against us. The judge will choose the other side's arguments. The client won't hire us. And our colleagues won't show up to our CLEs or refer us to other people.

A great example of this can be seen in the 1986 Frontline documentary *Inside the Jury Room*, which gives a rare look inside jury deliberations from a real case. Both principles—wanting to get home and to do a good job—are at the center of their discussion.

Here's how one juror in the documentary summarized his feelings about the case:

> In spite of this awesome room and these very serious people, and in spite of their lovely dog and pony show with the legal rigamarole, I'm sort of sitting to myself thinking, this is Mickey Mouse. I mean I really don't feel that this is a justified expenditure of my time and attention as a juror.[3]

To put this advice in more practical terms:

- A **closing argument** to a jury should not be about what a great case we put on or how clever our legal maneuvers were. It should be about why they should vote for our client, how they can reach their verdict quickly, and why they should feel good about it. In my experience, whenever I start talking about what the jurors need to know or do is when they start taking notes. If you look back at the example of the "knowledge-gap" closing in Section 1.2, each question to the jury focuses on information to help the jury do its job. This is one way to make the closing about them, not us.
- An **oral argument** should not be about how clever we are, how well we know the cases, or how foolish the other side's position is. It should be about the quickest path for the court to resolve this case and feel good about it, so it can move on to the next one and eventually get home.

3. *Inside the Jury Room* (PBS Frontline 1986), https://www.youtube.com/watch?v=Enkf4OXZa0A.

- A **client meeting** should not be about showing off how impressive we are, the results we got in other cases, or our prestigious pedigree. It should be about showing that we understand the client, we understand their problem, and we know how to quickly solve it.
- A **CLE** should not be about how accomplished we are, how many cases we've won, or how much information we know. It should be about sharing knowledge that will help our audience in their daily lives and practice.

We can also show the audience that the presentation is about them by using language that brings them into the conversation. I'm talking about language that breaks the wall, acknowledges they are in the room, and changes the dynamic from a person talking *at* them to a person conversing *with* them.

When transitioning between topics, don't say, "Now *I* want to talk about ______." Say, "This takes *us* to another point," or "now let *us* talk about ______."

Rather than saying "my client presented evidence that showed ______," say "*we* all saw the evidence showed ______."

It helps to think of us less as presenters delivering information and more as guides taking the audience on a collective journey. According to research by psychologist Robert Cialdini, we are also more persuasive when we use language that suggests we are part of the same group as our audience. For example, in one study, a young woman who asked for donations on a college campus received significantly more donations when she added the phrase, "I'm a student here, too," to her request. Cialdini calls this the "unity" principle of persuasion. It says that the more someone perceives the speaker to share an identity with them, the more likely the person is to connect with and be influenced by the speaker. Try saying "we" and "us" more in your next talk and see if you get more engagement.

In the end, make it all about the audience.

Quick Tip from a Transactional Lawyer

Michael Davis is a managing shareholder in Greenberg Traurig's Los Angeles Office, where he focuses on real estate transactions. I asked him for a tip about communicating with clients and deal partners in the corporate setting. Here is what he said:

Get to the point and tell the client what you think. We distill complex legal issues into discrete decisions for our clients—we aren't law professors. Frame the decision, advise your client, and then do your best to make their decision work for them.

When it comes to negotiations, it's all about tone and approach. Remember that you were hired to get a deal done, not to fight or show everyone how smart you are. Even if things get adversarial, your job is to create a collaborative environment and find solutions. This makes the job fun and gets you repeat business (from your client and maybe even the other side).

* * *

I told you every audience wants to feel good. This is based on the idea that everyone always cares about their own happiness. Hopefully I don't need to give you a research paper to convince you of this.

It's an old idea. In Aristotle's famous treatise on public speaking, *Rhetoric*, he wrote "[i]t may be said that every individual man and all men in common aim at a certain end which determines what they choose and what they avoid. This end, to sum it up briefly, is happiness. . . ."[4]

This means it pays to make the audience feel happy in our presentations. We can do this several ways. We can entertain them, because people are happy when they are entertained. (But don't let the entertainment interfere with anything else they came for because that will frustrate them.)

We can inspire them—meaning we can show them a brighter future is possible (for themselves or their community), which is a happy thing to think about.

And we can make them feel important. People are happy when they feel important because it indicates status, which our ancestors linked to longevity and survival. It also shows their lives have meaning, which all humans want.

4. Aristotle, Rhetoric (W. Rhys Roberts trans.), https://classics.mit.edu/Aristotle/rhetoric.mb.txt.

EXAMPLE: *DEPP V. HEARD*

The closing arguments from the Johnny Depp / Amber Heard defamation trial show us a good example of making jurors feel happy about their decision.

In her closing argument, Depp's lawyer Camille Vasquez gave the jurors a chance to feel like they could deliver something good with a verdict for Depp, and in turn feel important and happy. She told them that they could give Depp "his life back."

Here's how she started:

> On May 27th, 2016, Ms. Heard walked into a courthouse in Los Angeles, California, to get a no notice, *ex parte* restraining order against Mr. Depp and in doing so ruined his life by falsely telling the world that she was a survivor of domestic abuse at the hands of Mr. Depp. Today, on May 27th, 2022, exactly six years later, we ask you to give Mr. Depp his life back by telling the world that Mr. Depp is not the abuser that Ms. Heard said he is....[5]

Later, she told them that they "have been entrusted with a serious task. What is at stake in this trial is a man's good name. Even more than that, what is at stake in this trial is a man's life. The life he lost when he was accused of a heinous crime and the life he could live when he is finally vindicated."

In short, she framed a verdict for Depp as something for the jury to feel good about.

By contrast, Heard's lawyer did not give jurors a chance to feel happy about a verdict for Heard. He framed his pitch around negative emotions, and he only gave them the chance to avoid feeling bad about their verdict.

He told the jury that if they voted for Depp, they would be sending a bad message to domestic violence victims everywhere—"If you didn't take pictures, it didn't happen." He told them that is what Depp was trying "to get you, the jury, to be an accomplice to."[6] In other words, they weren't

---

5. Camille Vasquez, Closing Argument (May 27, 2022), available at https://www.youtube.com/watch?app=desktop&v=7L0Jl0voe8U

6. Benjamin Rottenborn, Closing Argument (May 27, 2022), https://www.youtube.com/watch?v=QDbaqB7tfUY

there to do anything important; they were there to avoid being hoodwinked by the other side.

If you followed the trial, you know that Heard lost (she won a small counterclaim, but it was a net win for Depp). I'm not saying this framing is what won and lost the case. But I am saying it is something to observe, and that Vasquez did a better job giving the jurors a chance to feel happy and important.

With a few simple changes, Heard's lawyer could have done the same thing. Rather than talking about sending a bad message to victims everywhere, he could have told the jury that a vote for Heard would send an important message to people who feel victimized—that they shouldn't be afraid to speak.

I don't know if it would have changed the result, but it could have made him more persuasive in that moment.

2.2 Frame Your Message to Fit Their Values and Beliefs

This next idea is thousands of years old and has been confirmed by modern science. The idea is that people's values and beliefs influence their decisions. And that, as the messenger, we are more persuasive if we frame our message to speak to those values and beliefs.

Aristotle understood this when he wrote his treatise *Rhetoric* more than 2,000 years ago. He said, "We must also take into account the nature of our particular audience when making a speech.... If the audience esteems a given quality, we must say that our hero has that quality."[7]

Alexandre Auguste Ledru-Rollin—a leader in the 1848 French Revolution—understood this when he said (perhaps apocryphally), "There go my people. I must find out where they are going so I can lead them there."

Ruth Bader Ginsburg knew this when she was an ACLU lawyer arguing gender discrimination cases in the 1970s.

Knowing that she would face an all-male Supreme Court, she picked cases with male plaintiffs who suffered from gender stereotypes because they might

7. ARISTOTLE, cited above in note 4.

rouse more sympathy from the male justices.[8] She also chose her language carefully to keep her male audience on task. Justice Ginsburg explained that she used the phrase "gender discrimination" instead of "sex discrimination" in her arguments because when nine men heard "sex," their first association would not be what she wanted them to think about.[9] In short, she knew her audience.

Around the same time, social science started confirming that framing makes a big difference in how messages are received. In the 1970s and 80s, psychologists Amos Tversky and Daniel Kahneman found that people made different decisions about the same sets of facts based on how they were framed.[10] One study found that more participants chose to treat lung cancer with surgery when they were told it had a 90% "survival rate" instead of a 10% "mortality rate."[11] The core information was the same; the framing was different. This led Kahneman to conclude, "People don't choose between things, they choose between descriptions of things."[12]

These takeaways are helpful when paired with research from psychologist Robert Cialdini in the 1980s and 90s. He found that people behave consistent with their attitudes and beliefs, and that they are more easily persuaded if the messenger taps into those attitudes and beliefs.[13]

In his best-selling book *Influence*, Cialdini writes that "[o]nce we have made a choice or taken a stand, we will encounter personal and interpersonal pressures to behave consistently with that commitment."[14] And those pres-

---

8. Neil A. Lewis, *The Supreme Court: Woman in the News; Rejected as a Clerk, Chosen as a Justice: Ruth Joan Bader Ginsburg*, N.Y. Times, June 15, 1993; Melissa Block, *Pathmarking The Way: Ruth Bader Ginsburg's Lifelong Fight for Gender Equality*, NPR (Sept. 24, 2020), https://www.npr.org/2020/09/24/916377135/pathmarking-the-way-ruth-bader-ginsburgs-lifelong-fight-for-gender-equality.

9. Block, cited above in note 8.

10. Amos Tversky & Daniel Kahneman, *The Framing of Decisions and the Psychology of Choice*, 211 Sci. 453 (1981); Amos Tversky & Daniel Kahneman, *Rational Choice and the Framing of Decisions*, 59 J. Bus. S251 (1986).

11. Tversky & Kahneman, *Rational Choice and the Framing of Decisions*, cited above in note 10.

12. He eventually won the Nobel Prize for this research in 2002. Tversky would have won it too if he were still alive at the time. Cass R. Sunstein & Richard H. Thaler, *The Two Friends Who Changed How We Think About How We Think*, New Yorker, Dec. 7, 2016.

13. *See, e.g.*, Robert B. Cialdini, Melanie R. Trost & Jason T. Newsom, *Preference for Consistency: The Development of a Valid Measure and the Discovery of Surprising Behavioral Implications*, 69 J. Personality & Soc. Psych. 318 (1995).

14. Robert B. Cialdini, Influence 57 (rev. ed. 2006).

sures will force us to justify our earlier position, so much that we "fool ourselves from time to time in order to keep our thoughts and beliefs consistent with what we have already done or decided."[15]

In 2015, psychologists Matthew Feinberg and Robb Willer put these two ideas—framing and consistency—together.

In six studies, they found that people's attitudes towards political issues could be nudged if the policies were reframed around their values. For example, conservatives accepted same-sex marriage more when the argument for it was framed around the conservative value of loyalty (same-sex couples are proud and patriotic Americans) versus the liberal value of fairness (all citizens should be treated equally).

Similarly, liberals became more accepting of military spending when the argument for it was framed around the liberal value of fairness (the military gives disadvantaged people the chance to overcome poverty and inequality) versus the conservative value of loyalty (the military ensures the United States is the greatest nation in the world).[16]

Again, two things mattered—the description of the thing (framing) and the audience's pre-existing beliefs (consistency).

Cognitive psychologist Eryn Newman—from the University of California-Irvine—explains: "The less effort it takes to process a factual claim, the more accurate it seems. When we fluidly and frictionlessly absorb a piece of information, one that perhaps snaps neatly into our existing belief structures, we are filled with a sense of comfort, familiarity, and trust."[17]

And other "researchers have been wisely noting for over 50 years [that] when faced with a communication that is either boring or runs counter to their own attitudes or beliefs, most people are adept at either tuning out, turning off, or simply refusing to expose themselves to that message."[18]

Law schools are starting to teach this.

In a talk on persuasion, University of Michigan law professor Sherman J. Clark explains, "Persuasion is not about the abstract, logical strength of your

---

15. *Id.* at 58.

16. Matthew Feinberg & Robb Willer, *From Gulf to Bridge: When Do Moral Arguments Facilitate Political Influence?*, 41 Personality & Soc. Psych. Bull. 1665 (2015).

17. Katy Waldman, *The Science of Truthiness*, SLATE (Sept. 3, 2014), https://slate.com/technology/2014/09/truthiness-research-cognitive-biases-for-simple-clear-conservative-messages.html.

18. Elliot Aronson, *The Power of Self-Persuasion*, 54 Am. Psychologist 875 (1999).

argument." Instead, it "is better understood as a process of trying to find or make space for your outcome, your understanding, in the world view of a particular person you are trying to reach. You've got to figure out, understand, and speak to, what actually matters to them."[19]

He calls this having "cognitive empathy."

Great lawyers have it and use it to their advantage. Let's look at two great examples.

EXAMPLE 1: TED OLSON'S ARGUMENT FOR SAME-SEX MARRIAGE TO CONSERVATIVES

In 2008, California voters passed Proposition 8 to amend the state constitution to ban same-sex marriage. Lawyers quickly moved to overturn it as unconstitutional under the Fourteenth Amendment of the federal Constitution.

Headlines were made when an unlikely advocate joined their team—Theodore Olson, former United States Solicitor General under President George W. Bush. When Olson joined the case, he realized it was not only important to persuade the court, but also his conservative friends.

He wrote an article in Newsweek titled, *The Conservative Case for Gay Marriage.*[20] It noted that his involvement in the case generated consternation among conservatives. "How could a politically active, lifelong Republican, and veteran of the Ronald Reagan and George W. Bush administrations, challenge the 'traditional' definition of marriage and press for an 'activist' interpretation of the Constitution to create another 'new' constitutional right?"

To answer this, Olson started by explaining that same-sex marriage "promote[s] the values conservatives prize." He wrote:

> Marriage is one of the basic building blocks of our neighborhoods and our nation. At its best, it is a stable bond between two individuals who work to create a loving household and a social and economic partnership. We encourage couples

19. Sherman J. Clark, *Arguably Better: Empathy and Persuasion*, Mich. L. Video Lecture Series (July 19, 2024), https://www.youtube.com/watch?v=7uIyil5cqps

20. Theodore B. Olson, *The Conservative Case for Gay Marriage*, Newsweek, Jan. 8, 2010.

> to marry because the commitments they make to one another provide benefits not only to themselves but also to their families and communities.... The fact that individuals who happen to be gay want to share in this vital social institution is evidence that conservative ideals enjoy widespread acceptance. Conservatives should celebrate this, rather than lament it.

I doubt this persuaded everyone in his audience, but I'm sure it connected with some. And it probably connected a lot better than if Olson had started arguing about equality. Olson's public advocacy also aligned with a dramatic increase in public support for same-sex marriage.[21] Perhaps his message contributed to that.

The point is Olson understood two things: (1) who his audience was and (2) how to speak to what mattered to them.

EXAMPLE 2: JOHN HUESTON'S OPENING IN *KOCH V. GREENBERG*

This example doesn't involve a polarizing social issue. Instead, it's about making an extraordinary situation relatable to everyday jurors.

In *Koch v. Greenberg*, John Hueston represented a billionaire wine collector who was suing a wine merchant for selling him $300,000 of counterfeit wine. Hueston recognized that on the surface, the case did not have a lot of jury appeal.

He had to think hard about how he was going to frame the case, starting with the opening statement. Hueston later wrote: "The goal was to make a billionaire who spent the kind of money on wine that most people spent on a home sympathetic to the judge and the initially skeptical New York jury."[22]

These were his opening lines at trial:

> This is a simple case about a seller who failed to disclose information any buyer would want to know before spending thou-

21. *See* Ctr. for Am. Progress, *The Evolution of Support for Marriage Equality: A Majority of Americans Now Support Marriage Equality*, Center for American Progress (June 16, 2011), https://americanprogress.org/article/the-evolution-of-support-for-marriage-equality.

22. John Hueston., *Art of the Trial: The Opening Statement*, L.A. Daily J., Sept. 19, 2016.

> sands of dollars.... This seller knew of problems, concerns and issues with bottles in that collection; problems, concern and issues that made those bottles worthless or nearly worthless for sale. We're here because that seller didn't tell the buyer about any of those problems, issues and concerns.

Hueston explains his strategy:

> I didn't talk about wine, and never mentioned that my client was a billionaire. I focused on collecting and the honesty a buyer looks for in a seller. That's true whether the collector is purchasing stamps, autographed baseballs, coin books—or fine wine. The ultimate goal is for jurors to consider your client's dilemma and conclude, "There but for the grace of God go I."

Just like Olson, Hueston knew two things: (1) who his audience was and (2) how to talk to them.

The next time you prepare a speech or argument, use this tool to make the persuasive hill you need to climb smaller—or the distance you are asking your audience to travel shorter.

If you are a prosecutor trying a case to jurors who may be skeptical of police, don't argue that police officers are trustworthy people. Instead, acknowledge that we've seen too many cases of bad police officers in the news, but argue that is not a good reason to punish police officers who do a good job. Framed this way, you are speaking to jurors from their side of the issue. You are asking them to travel a smaller distance to accept your point.

If you are a plaintiff's lawyer asking for noneconomic damages in a conservative venue, don't ask the jury to award damages to ease your client's pain and suffering and make their life easier. Instead, ask them to award damages to repay what the defendant stole—a life free from pain. With conservative jurors who think life is hard for everyone, but who also hate stealing, this might make a difference.

Framing won't decide every case, but it will make a difference in a lot of them. Thus, great lawyers must master the art of framing.

Quick Tip from an Advocate

Cristyn Chadwick is a Senior Counsel at Eisner LLP—a business and entertainment firm in Los Angeles. She has extensive experience representing colorful clients in broad-ranging disputes. I asked her for a tip about tailoring your message to your audience. This is what she said:

> I recently represented the owner of a bookkeeping firm at a jury trial. The plaintiff was an heiress to a ski resort fortune and sued my client for professional negligence, claiming he negligently hired and supervised an employee, who embezzled significant funds from her.
>
> We were facing an uphill battle since the employee had already been convicted of felony embezzlement and was in jail. The trial was before a rural jury. Even though the plaintiff claimed a 10-figure damage number, I knew the jury would pay more attention to whether my client was an honest, hardworking guy than to experts fighting over damage calculations.
>
> I asked every defense witness (employees, clients, family members) the exact same final question—whether they believed my client did right by his clients and did his best to serve them. Every witness gave honest, but subtly compelling, answers. In closing, I asked the jury to reach the same conclusion that every witness already reached—even if that conclusion was, legally, mostly beside the point. We won a full defense verdict because I knew what my jury wanted to hear, and I gave them an opportunity to lean into it.

2.3 Make Them Think It Before You Say It

Since we're still inside our audience's mind, it's time to discuss the "paradox of persuasion." The late trial advocacy professor James McElhaney explains it like this:

> The more you argue—the harder you push—the more the judge and jury resist what you say. "Why?" Because no one likes to be told how to think. People like their own ideas. Your job is to be a guide. To show, not tell. Use your closing to give the fact finders what they need—the right stories and pictures—to help them make up their own minds the right way.[23]

Just like our last idea, great thinkers have thought this for a long time.

In the 17th century, French philosopher Blaise Pascal wrote: "People are usually more convinced by reasons they discovered themselves than by those found out by others."

Centuries later, President Dwight D. Eisenhower said: "Leadership is the art of getting someone else to do something you want done because he wants to do it."

More recently, in his best-selling book, *Never Split the Difference*, former FBI hostage negotiator Chris Voss wrote: "Persuasion is not about how bright or smooth or forceful you are. It's about the other party convincing themselves that the solution you want is their own idea."

Modern psychologists call this phenomenon "self-persuasion." They have confirmed, over and over, that it is real.

Psychologist Elliot Aronson—recipient of the lifetime achievement award from the Association of Psychological Science—knows as much about it as anybody else.

He wrote: "The common theme running through my 40 years of research appears to be the phenomenon of self-persuasion and its enormous power to affect long-term changes in attitudes and behavior."[24]

He tells us that "[s]elf-persuasion is almost always a more powerful form of persuasion ... than more traditional persuasion techniques—that is, than being directly persuaded by another person, no matter how clever, convinc-

23. James W. McElhaney, *Great Arguments*, A.B.A. J., Mar. 2004, at 48.
24. Aronson, cited above in note 18.

ing, expert, and trustworthy that other person might be—precisely because in direct persuasion, the audience is constantly aware of the fact that they have been persuaded by another." But when self-persuasion happens "people are convinced that the motivation for change has come from within."

The best trial lawyers strive to persuade people this way. In the HBO docuseries *Body in the Snow: The Trial of Karen Read*, defense attorney Alan Jackson explained his approach to closing arguments like this:

> If you are savvy enough to present the facts, you don't have to bludgeon the jurors to death with your interpretation of the facts. I want them to say it in their mind before I say it with my mouth. I want them to come to that conclusion themselves. That's the power of a good closing.[25]

Long-time California trial court judge Gregory W. Alarcon agrees. He says, "The goal of any closing argument is to create 'aha' moments in the minds of the jurors where information is layered in argument crafted in such a way that, like an outstanding professor, the students are convinced that the insights obtained were solely a product of the jurors' own thinking process."[26]

How do we do this? How do we make jurors and judges think our ideas are theirs?

Facts.

Facts force people to draw inferences and conclusions on their own. And when we control the facts they will focus on—and how those facts are presented—we can control the inferences they will draw.

But if we litter our presentation with adverbs and adjectives, we inject our own opinions and make it obvious that we're telling the jury how to think. And they don't like being told how to think.

This is a variation of the age-old advice "show, don't tell." Facts—think nouns and verbs—show. Opinions—think adjectives and adverbs—tell.

The secret to persuasive advocacy is selecting the right facts and then presenting them in the right order to compel the jury to reach your conclusion. And in the courtroom, where most jurors believe their job is to decide who did something wrong, it is usually best to lead with facts about your opponent's conduct (not your client's) to ensure that the jury is focusing their judgment in the direction you want.

25. "A Body in the Snow," *The Trial of Karen Read* (Episode 5, at 22 min.) (2025).

26. Gregory W. Alarcon, *Winston Churchill: Ideal Mentor for Trial Lawyers*, ADVOCATE, July 2017.

Let's say you have a car crash case and you want to show that the defendant was negligent when he ran a red light because the driving conditions were clear and nothing but negligence could have caused him to run the red. Rather than telling the jury that the conditions were "clear" (an adjective), it's better to show them that by saying something like:

> Let me take you to the moment of the crash. It was noon on a summer day in southern California. 82 degrees. No clouds in the sky. The sun was overhead. The defendant was driving north to meet with a client. The meeting was scheduled to start in 5 minutes, and the defendant was 10 minutes away. The light was red for the north/south traffic at this intersection, and the defendant drove through that red light at 55 miles per hour. At the same time, my client and his family happened to be in the middle of that intersection.

Rather than telling the jury the conditions were clear, this gives them the facts to draw the conclusion on their own. And it puts the focus on the defendant—not your client. The passage consists entirely of facts, yet anyone listening to it would form the opinion that the defendant was reckless.

Every story can be told from multiple angles. The job of a good advocate is to find the most persuasive angle to tell it for your client and then to do it using mostly facts.

If you're defending a personal injury case, you can use the same tools of persuasion. Let's say you believe the plaintiff is faking or exaggerating their injuries. Just saying that to the jury is not persuasive, and it may even turn them off. On the other hand, if you never say it, but point to facts that show it, you can persuade the jury to accept it on their own. For example, pointing out that the plaintiff was walking fine after the accident, did not visit a doctor for a month, only saw the doctor their lawyer hired, and never took any pain meds stronger than Advil. Simply hearing these facts will make the jurors question the plaintiff's claims.

Now let's look at a great real-life example from the 2021 George Floyd murder trial.[27]

27. *Minnesota v. Chauvin*, opening statement, Mar. 29, 2021, transcript available at https://www.famous-trials.com/george-floyd/2718-opening-arguments-in-the-george-floyd-murder-chauvin-trial.

EXAMPLE 1: GEORGE FLOYD MURDER TRIAL

In his opening statement, prosecutor Jerry Blackwell—now a federal judge—set out to show that Minneapolis police officer Derek Chauvin used excessive force without regard for George Floyd's life when he kneeled on Floyd's neck and killed him.

To do this, he painted a picture with facts that he told the jurors they could see and hear them for themselves.

> So let's begin by focusing then on what we will learn about this nine minutes and 29 seconds. And you will be able to hear Mr. Floyd saying, "Please, I can't breathe, please, man, please." In this nine minutes and 29 seconds you will see that as Mr. Floyd is handcuffed there on the ground, he is verbalizing 27 times you will hear in the four minutes and 45 seconds, "I can't breathe, please. I can't breathe." You will see that Mr. Chauvin is kneeling on Mr. Floyd's neck and back.
>
> He has one knee on his neck and the knee on his back is intermittently off and on, on his back as you will be able to see for yourself in the video footage. You will hear Mr. Floyd as he's crying out. You hear him at some point, cry out for his mother when he's being squeezed. He was very close to his mother, you will learn. You will hear him say, "Tell my kids I love them." You will hear him say about his fear of dying, he says, "I'll probably die this way. I'm through. I'm through. They're going to kill me. They're going to kill me, man."
>
> You will hear him crying out and you will hear him cry out in pain, "My stomach hurts. My neck hurts. Everything hurts." You will hear that for yourself, "Please. I can't breathe. Please, your knee on my neck." You will hear it and you'll see at the same time, while he's crying out, Mr. Chauvin never moves. The knee remains on his neck. Sunglasses remain undisturbed on his head and it just goes on. You will hear his final words when he says, "I can't breathe." Before that time, you'll hear his voice get heavier. You will hear his words further apart. You will see that his respiration gets shallower and shallower, and finally stops when he speaks his last words, "I can't breathe." …
>
> During this period of time, you will learn that Mr. Chauvin is told that they can't even find the pulse of Mr. Floyd. You'll learn

> he's told that twice. They can't even find the pulse. You will be able to see for yourself what he does in response. You will see that he does not let up and that he does not get up. Even when Mr. Floyd does not even have a pulse, it continues on, it continues on ladies and gentlemen, even after the ambulance arrives on the scene. The ambulance is there and you'll be able to see for yourself what Mr. Chauvin is doing when the ambulance is there. You can compare. You'll be able to compare how he looks in this photograph to how he looked in the first four minutes and 45 seconds.
>
> Same position. Doesn't let up and you'll see he doesn't get up. The paramedic from the ambulance comes over, you'll be able to see this in the video, he checks Mr. Floyd for a pulse. He has to check him for a pulse you'll see, with Mr. Chauvin continuing to remain on his body at the same time, doesn't get up even when the paramedic comes to check for a pulse and doesn't find one, Mr. Chauvin doesn't get up. You will see that the paramedics have taken the gurney out of the ambulance, have rolled it over next to the body of Mr. Floyd and you'll be able to see Mr. Chauvin still does not let up, he doesn't get up.

Notice the following.

First, Blackwell doesn't *tell* the jury that Chauvin was indifferent to Floyd's life. He *shows* it.

They hear that Floyd said he couldn't breathe twenty-seven times while "Mr. Chauvin never moves. The knee remains on his neck. Sunglasses remain undisturbed on his head."

It is a great example of painting a visual picture. The image of Chauvin kneeling with the sunglasses undisturbed on his head—paired with Floyd's actual words—makes it feel real, like they are living it. Blackwell also accomplishes this by using the present tense, as if the jurors are bystanders watching it happen.

Second, notice how many times Blackwell emphasizes that these are things the jurors will see and hear for themselves. With the words "you will see" and "you will hear," Black invites the jurors to invoke their senses. These aren't things they are being told; these are things they are experiencing in their minds.

Third, in this passage, he never says "I will prove" or "the State will prove." Instead, everything is phrased to be a collective experience with the jurors. He begins focusing on "what we will learn." The jurors aren't going to be passive recipients of information. Blackwell makes them feel like they will be the central figures in the trial, and that he is simply their guide.

He makes them feel like it will be about them.

Another "show, don't tell" technique attorneys use to persuade juries is turning the other side's words against them. The idea is that because the other side said it, they can't dispute it. You get twice as many points when it comes from your opponent's mouth. We will see this in the next example, where the attorney doesn't just tell the jury what the other side said, he shows it to them.

EXAMPLE 2: *UNITED STATES V. BACA*

For decades, inmates in Los Angeles County jails alleged they were being abused by the sheriff's deputies working them. The ACLU got involved, and then in the early 2010s, federal authorities started their own investigation. This eventually led to an attempted cover-up by high-ranking members of the Sheriff's Department, including the Sheriff himself, Leroy Baca.

The U.S. Attorney's Office charged Baca with participating in the conspiracy, which involved multiple obstructive acts. Baca took the case to trial. The main issue was how much he knew about the interference, since most of the conduct was committed by people below him. Baca predictably tried to shift blame to those people, particularly his Undersheriff Paul Tanaka.

In the government's opening statement, federal prosecutor Brandon Fox erased questions of Baca's ignorance by repeatedly using Baca's own words against him. And he didn't just tell jurors what Baca said in the past, he showed it to them, playing four different excerpts of Baca's deposition testimony from prior cases. This included testimony where Baca said his relationship with Tanaka was like "father and son," that he "handpicked" Tanaka and "raised him through the ranks," and that Tanaka "had a unique talent of doing exactly what I wanted done."

Baca also once referred to the interactions with the feds as a "chess match." Fox turned this into a theme. One of the obstructive acts alleged was that the Sheriff's Department moved an FBI informant to different jail cells to hide him from the feds. Fox cleverly tied this to Baca's "chess match" statement, telling jurors that Baca "was trying to move pieces in order to force the federal government to back down and stop its federal grand jury investigation."

This was a strong theme, and it worked particularly well because it was based on Baca's words. The jury did not have to think too much about its fit because Baca said it himself, as they saw and heard.

Fox is now the managing partner of Jenner & Block's Los Angeles Office. I asked him to tell me more about his strategy at trial. This is what he said:

> There is no more compelling evidence than the opposing party's own words. By using them in opening and building them into my themes, I know that when the jury hears those words again as they come in as evidence during trial, the jury will understand the words' implication and importance.

2.4 Use Inclusive Language and Examples

Consumer surveys show that people trust brands more when they feel represented in their marketing. Carrying this over to speaking, it means our audience will trust and connect with us more if we use language and examples that include them. If we don't, some people will feel excluded—or worse, alienated—by our presentation and turn away from our message.

This often happens when speakers use gendered language that reflects past stereotypes about what genders played what roles in society—for example, saying policeman instead of police officer. In short, "gendered language" assumes a person's gender when it isn't relevant.

It rarely comes from a bad place—often it's habit or tradition. And some people don't mind it. But others do, so it is worth paying attention to. It all comes down to having empathy for our audience. Using gender-neutral alternatives seldom hurts anyone, and it ensures everyone in the audience feels included.

Below is a chart of gendered terms that commonly appear in legal settings, next to easy-to-say neutral alternatives. It can be hard to adopt them all overnight, but with practice they become second nature.

Gendered vs. Neutral Language in Legal Settings

Context	Gendered	Neutral
Job titles	policeman, businessman, salesman, chairman, congressman, spokesman	police officer, business owner / professional, salesperson / sales rep, chair / chairperson, member of congress / representative, spokesperson
Jury	ladies and gentlemen of the jury, foreman	members of the jury / jurors, foreperson
Hypos	if a reasonable man were in this situation	if a reasonable person were in this situation
Groups	you guys	everyone, you all, folks
Instructions	each expert should bring his CV	each expert should bring their CV

3

Rule Three: Have a Memorable Through Line

Time for more hard truths about our audiences. They can only process a limited amount of information at any one time.[1] When their brains get overloaded, they shut down. They have bad memories.

In 2013, neuroscientist Carmen Simon invited 1,500 people to view a 20-slide PowerPoint presentation with one message per slide. Two days later, she asked what they remembered. On average, people remembered four slides, and mostly at random (meaning different people remembered different things).[2] With some participants, Simon tried to make certain slides stand out from the rest. In that group, they still remembered four slides on average, but at least they remembered the slides she emphasized.

In *Impossible to Ignore*, Simon explains that "[p]eople act on what they remember, not on what they forget."[3] And the problem is not just that people remember very little, it is that they "remember very little *at random,*" unless you take control of the small bit they will remember.[4] Thus, Simon writes, the memorable presenter "practices content restraint and has a strong 10% message" that the audience will remember.[5]

1. Richard E. Mayer, Multimedia Learning 36 (3d ed. 2021).
2. Carmen Simon, Impossible to Ignore 87 (2016).
3. *Id.* at 28.
4. *Id.* at 86–87.
5. *Id.* at 86.

In other words, we need to simplify and emphasize our core message to help it get through.

Other presentation experts agree.

The Heath brothers say, "If you say three things, you don't say anything."[6]

Valerie Madamba, "The Legal Presentation Coach," says if you cannot "[s]ummarize the point of your session in one sentence ... you don't have a presentation. You have a series of lists."[7]

Bill McGowan says, "Good communication is a lot like pasta sauce. The more you boil down and reduce a sauce, the more dynamic the flavor."[8]

In the *Harvard Business Review*, public speaker John Coleman writes that every presentation needs a "clear thesis stated up front so that listeners can easily follow and interpret the comments that follow."[9] "I can't tell you how many times I've seen business presenters ramble through a speech with the audience wondering to the very end about the point of the comments."

John Hueston says, "At the conclusion of trial, jurors rarely articulate more than four or five grounds for a conviction; most of the trial's evidence washes over a jury that will likely seize only a few 'decision moments' from the proceedings."[10]

In *Winning at Persuasion*, trial lawyer Shane Read writes, "You need to be able to concisely state in one sentence why you should win and why it matters."[11]

Chief Justice Roberts says, "In five minutes if you can't explain what's this case about and why you should win" to a layperson, you've got to practice your argument again.[12]

We have a consensus here.

Research supports it too.

In 2017, London Business School professor Niro Sivanathan published a study where he gave thousands of participants information about a drug's side

---

6. Heath & Heath, cited above in Chapter 1, note 17, at 34.

7. Valerie Madamba, February 2025 LinkedIn Post.

8. McGowan, cited above in Chapter 1, note 6, at 80.

9. John Coleman, *5 Tips for Off-the-Cuff Speaking*, Harv. Bus. Rev. (Aug. 29, 2014), https://hbr.org/2014/08/5-tips-for-off-the-cuff-speaking.

10. Hueston, cited above in Chapter 1, note 5.

11. Shane Read, Winning at Persuasion for Lawyers: The Art and Science of Public Speaking at Hearings and Trials 48 (2021).

12. Bryan A. Garner, *Interview with Chief Justice John G. Roberts*, Jr., 13 Scribes J. Legal Writing 5, 25 (2010).

effects.[13] He told half the group about only the severe side effects, and he told the other half about both the severe and moderate side effects. He found that this second group—the one told about both the severe and moderate side effects—rated the overall severity of the drug significantly lower than the first group that was told about only the severe effects.

Professor Sivanathan attributes this to a cognitive bias called the "dilution effect"—where less-important information dilutes the value of more-important information.

In a later TED Talk, he explained:

> What this body of research tells us is that in the world of communicating for the purposes of influence, quality trumps quantity. By increasing the number of arguments, you do not strengthen your case, but rather you actively weaken it.... Stick to your strong arguments, because your arguments don't add up in the minds of the receiver, they average out.[14]

In short, we need to prioritize our most important points and have a plan to make sure they get through, if nothing else.

* * *

The best way to do this is with a "through line."

A through line is a single theme or idea that runs from the beginning to the end of something—be it a book, movie, news article, or presentation. It works for two reasons.

First, it helps the audience follow along by giving them one big idea to which they can attach all the other information they are presented. If they know the message, they can place the details in context and see why they are important and not just random bits of information.

Brain scientist John Medina tells us that the "brain processes meaning before detail."[15] People need "the general idea *first*."[16] "Start with the key ideas and, in a hierarchical fashion, form the details around these larger notions."[17]

---

13. Niro Sivanathan & Hemant Kakkar, *The Unintended Consequences of Argument Dilution in Direct-to-Consumer Drug Advertisements*, 1 NATURE HUM. BEHAV. 797 (2017).

14. Niro Sivanathan, *The Counterintuitive Way to be More Persuasive*, TED Talk (May 2019), https://www.ted.com/talks/niro_sivanathan_the_counterintuitive_way_to_be_more_persuasive?subtitle=en.

15. MEDINA, cited above in Chapter 1, note 13, at 90.

16. *Id.*

17. *Id.* at 84.

This lines up with research by educational psychologist Richard Mayer. In study after study, he saw that learners performed better on tests when the presenter directed their attention to the essential material in the presentation.[18]

Second, by giving a clear meaning to our presentation, a through line also makes it more memorable. This is because our brains are better at keeping "gist memories" (the general meaning of something) than "verbatim memories" (accurate, detailed representations).[19] Thus, it pays to have a clear and compelling gist.

The TED Talk organization champions through lines. Their official guide says, "Every talk should have one."[20] They want you to think of it "as a strong cord or rope, onto which you will attach all the elements that are part of the idea you are building."[21]

Good lawyers are proponents too. Judge Alarcon writes that all trials should have them "to assist jurors in understanding the case and lawyers in preparing them."[22]

So what makes a good through line?

No one formula exists, but it should capture as much of our core message as possible in a punchy, succinct way. In a trial, it should capture the strongest reason we should win. Sometimes it can be built around one key piece of evidence, or a few related pieces. Think of it like a trump card in the jury room. If one juror starts talking about a reason we shouldn't win, our take-home message should be something the other jurors can say that immediately shifts the conversation back to us winning.

In an oral argument, it should be the point we'd expect to see at the top of the court's opinion explaining why we won. Late appellate lawyer John W. Davis called it going for "the jugular vein."[23] He explained that in every case, there is usually "a cardinal point around which lesser points revolve like planets around the sun ...; a central fortress which if strongly held will make the loss of all the outworks immaterial."

---

18. Mayer, cited above in note 1, at 166–167.

19. Simon, cited above in note 2, at 92; Medina, cited above in Chapter 1, note 13, at 83 ("our retrieval of gist always trumps our recall of details").

20. Chris Anderson, TED Talks: The Official TED Guide to Public Speaking 61 (2016).

21. *Id.*

22. Alarcon, cited above in Chapter 2, note 26.

23. John W. Davis, *The Argument of an Appeal*, 3 J. App. Prac. & Process 745 (2001).

In a CLE, it should be the one unique thought we want the audience to take home and incorporate in their practice, if nothing else.

In a client meeting, it should be the one reason they should hire us, and not anyone else, to solve their problem.

To be memorable, it also helps when our through line is clever in an original way. This means it cannot be cliché because clichés are boring. Surprise, on the other hand, is interesting.[24]

For example, in Chapter 1, I talked about grabbing attention and told the story about how I use a Super Soaker to start out some public speaking lessons. I then wrapped that story into my main message—start your talks with "Super-Soaker moments." Before the talk, no one knew what a "Super-Soaker moment" was—at least as it pertains to public speaking—but they will likely remember the term afterward because it is tied to a surprising experience they had. This shows that our through line can be built around novel conceptual vocabulary we create ourselves. Often these are the most memorable. We will see this in some of the examples below.

Once you know your through line, build the rest of your presentation around it. Emphasize it multiple times so the audience has no question what your take-home message is. Find a way for every extra piece of information you share to tie back to it. You will find that your audiences become more engaged, and your presentations more memorable.

EXAMPLE 1: JOHNNIE COCHRAN

Let's look at some good through lines, starting with the most famous legal through line of all—Johnnie Cochran's "if it doesn't fit, you must acquit," from the O.J. Simpson trial.

Many people are familiar with this line, but they haven't seen the entire passage in which it appears.

Here's how Cochran introduced it:

> And so as we look then at the timeline and the importance of this timeline, I want you to remember these words. Like the defining moment in this trial, the day Mr. Darden asked Mr. Simpson to try on those gloves and the gloves didn't fit, remember

---

24. Heath & Heath, cited above in Chapter 1, note 17, at 65 ("Surprise gets our attention."); Simon, cited above in note 2, at 137 ("surprise was the single most reliable predictor of staying on people's minds long enough for them to act in our favor").

> these words: if it doesn't fit, you must acquit. And we are going to be talking about that throughout.[25]

After this, Cochran repeats the phrase three more times, each time after discussing an inconsistency in the prosecution's argument. In one, Cochran notes that the prosecution claimed Simpson went into his house in bloody clothes and shoes, and then argues:

> You've seen this house. You've seen this carpet. If he went in that house with bloody shoes, with bloody clothes, with bloody hands, as they say, where's the blood on the doorknob, where's the blood on the light switch, where's the blood on the banister, where's the blood on the carpet.... It just doesn't fit. If it doesn't fit, you must acquit.

In another, he notes the prosecution argued Simpson put on a knit cap as a disguise. Then he argues:

> I was thinking last night about this case and their theory and how it didn't make any sense and how it didn't fit and how something is wrong. It occurred to me how they were going to come here, stand up here and tell you how O.J. Simpson was going to disguise himself. He was going to put on a knit cap and some dark clothes, and he was going to get in his white Bronco, this recognizable person, and go over and kill his wife. That's what they want you to believe. That's how silly their argument is. And I said to myself, maybe I can demonstrate this graphically. Let me show you something.
>
> This is a knit cap. Let me put this knit cap on (Indicating). You have seen me for a year. If I put this knit cap on, who am I? I'm still Johnnie Cochran with a knit cap. And if you looked at O.J. Simpson over there—and he has a rather large head—O.J. Simpson in a knit cap from two blocks away is still O.J. Simpson. It's no disguise. It's no disguise. It makes no sense. It doesn't fit. If it doesn't fit, you must acquit.

Cochran does five things that make his through line effective and memorable.

---

25. *People v. O.J. Simpson*, closing argument, Sept. 27, 1995, transcript available at https://famous-trials.com/simpson/1868-cochranclosing.

First, he uses it to capture multiple holes in the prosecution's case in a compact way. Many people think he was just talking about the gloves, but if we look at the argument, Cochran uses it as a through line to tie together several inconsistencies he saw in the evidence.

Second, when he introduces it, he tells the jury that it is something important he wants them to remember. He says "remember these words" twice before introducing the phrase the first time.

Third, he repeats it and comes back to it several times in the argument. There is an expression that "time is the measure of importance in the courtroom." Here, by repeating the phrase multiple times, Cochran emphasizes its importance. The jury knows this is his take-home point.

Fourth, it is clever in an original way because it has a nice rhythm and rhymes. It's unlikely anyone in the courtroom heard the expression before, yet it's instantly memorable.

Finally, Cochran taps into the "rhyme-as-reason" effect. Before explaining this, let me back up a bit.

Ancient Greeks—who created the art of rhetoric—understood that the "aesthetic" qualities of statements could improve their impact. Thus, they developed aesthetic devices to make statements more beautiful and thus more appealing. The Greeks had fancy names for them—anaphora, epistrophe, tricolon, asyndeton, chiasmus. They all bring musical qualities to the language, using rhythm, repetition, parallel structures, or rhyming.

German philosopher Friedrich Nietzsche put it like this: "the wisest among us are still occasionally fooled by rhythm—if only insofar as we sometimes consider an idea truer because it has a metrical form and presents itself with a divine spark and jump."[26]

Think of some of the most memorable phrases in history and culture:

- "Ask not what your country can do for you; ask what you can do for your country."
- "If you see something, say something."
- "We shall fight on the beaches, we shall fight on the landing grounds, we shall fight in the field and in the streets ..."
- "I came, I saw, I conquered."

26. Friedrich Nietzsche, The Gay Science 139–40 (Walter Kaufmann ed. & trans., Vintage Books 1974) (1887).

- "Government of the people, by the people, for the people."
- "An apple a day keeps the doctor away."
- "Birds of a feather flock together."

They all use rhetorical devices to achieve an aesthetic quality that makes them more memorable.

As with most ancient Greek speaking discoveries, modern science has again confirmed the Greeks were onto something.

In 2000, psychologists Matthew McGlone and Jessica Tofighbakhsh published a study that found participants perceived statements that rhymed to be more accurate than similar statements that did not.[27]

For example, more considered the rhyming statement "what sobriety conceals, alcohol reveals" to be more accurate than the non-rhyming counterpart "what sobriety conceals, alcohol unmasks." They call this the "rhyme-as-reason" effect. They suggest it works because rhyming statements are easier for the brain to process.

They also say that Cochran's famous line likely got a boost from this effect. They write: "We wonder how persuasive the jury might have found this proposition had Cochran proclaimed, 'If the gloves don't fit, you must find him not guilty!'"

Now, it would be unethical for lawyers to use this technique to sell a false or misleading message, but it is not unethical to package a good-faith message in a way that makes it easier for the audience to process.

In the end, Cochran landed the most famous through line of any trial. Studying how he did it gives us insights into how we can make our take-home messages more persuasive and memorable.

I recommend trying each of his techniques in your next presentation: (1) find a statement that can be a vehicle for most of what you plan to say, (2) highlight it when you introduce it, (3) repeat it multiple times by tying your subpoints back to it, (4) make it clever in an original way, and (5) give it a nice aesthetic quality.

---

27. M.S. McGlone & J. Tofighbakhsh, *Birds of a Feather Flock Conjointly (?): Rhyme as Reason in Aphorisms*, 11 Psychol. Sci. 424 (2000).

EXAMPLE 2: ONE OF MY OWN

This example comes from one of my own trials.

In 2022, I defended a famous punk rock band in an accounting lawsuit by a former drummer. The drummer was seeking millions of dollars of alleged unpaid royalties.

The case was set for a one-week bench trial. The plaintiff planned to call almost a dozen witnesses, including the band members, current and former business managers, personal managers, and experts.

It was going to be a lot of testimony for the court to sift through, and we thought most of it would be irrelevant.

In my opening, I came up with a through line to present our side's message in simple terms and focus the court on the reason we should win. I said:

> Your Honor, the plaintiff is going to call a lot of witnesses in this trial. **But in the end, the star witness is the contract.** Our clients have paid him everything he is entitled to, and every extra dollar he seeks is foreclosed by the contract.

In my closing argument, I repeated it and showed the court that we delivered on our promise. I went through each category of extra royalties the plaintiff claimed he was owed and showed why it failed under his contract.

This isn't the greatest through line of all time, but it illustrates several qualities of an effective one. First, it captures the reason my clients should win in one-sentence, together with our response to each witness the plaintiff would call—none of this testimony matters, it all comes down to the contract.

Second, I repeated it and tied all my later points back to it. And third, it's a little clever and unexpected. Technically, the contract is an exhibit, not a witness. But there is no such thing as a "star exhibit," so I stole the phrase "star witness" and personified the contract to make it a memorable phrase that stood out. People in the courtroom said they liked it.

EXAMPLE 3: THE KOBE BRYANT CRASH PHOTOS TRIAL

In January 2020, a tragic helicopter crash took the lives of Kobe Bryant, his daughter Gianna, and seven others. Afterwards, it came out that four Los Angeles County Sheriff deputies who responded to the crash took or shared inappropriate photos of the victims' remains on their phones.

Vanessa Bryant, together with a surviving family member of two other victims, sued the county for negligence and violating their constitutional right to privacy. The case went to trial, and the jury awarded the plaintiffs $31 million for their emotional distress from worrying that the photos could appear on the internet any time.

At trial, the defense's core argument was that although the photos were shared among some sheriff's deputies and firefighters after the crash, the photos had not surfaced publicly in the two and a half years since that story broke. Thus, they argued, the effort to delete them worked and the plaintiff's constitutional rights were not violated.

To overcome this, the plaintiffs needed to show that the core wrongdoers could not be trusted to ensure all copies had been destroyed and that the photos would not surface online in the future.

In his closing argument, Vanessa Bryant's attorney Craig Jennings Lavoie did this in a memorable way by using the same structure to describe what each wrongdoer had done.

One by one, he argued that each wrongdoer had (1) done a bad thing by taking and sharing the photos, (2) lied about it, and (3) destroyed evidence. Thus, none of them could be trusted. For example, after discussing one of the wrongdoer's bad acts, lies, and destruction, Lavoie asked the jury, "Should you believe [him] that he didn't ever show them to anyone else, that he didn't ever send them to anyone else? Imagine, imagine how Mrs. Bryant and Mr. Chester feel about their fate being in [his] hands."

By using the same structure for each wrongdoer—bad act, then lie, then destruction—Lavoie made the closing easy for the jury to follow and remember. The lesson for all of us here is that once we've found our central message, it pays to structure the entire argument around it. This helps highlight the message to make sure the jury remembers it, if nothing else.

EXAMPLE 4: ALEC BALDWIN "RUST" TRIAL

In July 2024, screen actor Alec Baldwin went to trial on a charge of involuntary manslaughter for discharging a loaded revolver that killed a cinematographer during the filming of the movie **Rust**. His defense was that he did not know the gun was loaded, that he was just acting, and that the crew members responsible for gun safety failed in their duties, not him. Still, the prosecution argued that Baldwin could be guilty of manslaughter because he didn't do a gun safety check with the armorer before handling the firearm. Thus, whether Baldwin should have done his own safety check was a central issue in the case.

Baldwin's lawyer Alex Spiro understood this. In his opening statement, he made the following take-home point abundantly clear: "Safety has to occur before the gun is placed in the actor's hands." Spiro repeated variations of this point throughout his opening, saying "the gun has to be safe before it gets into the actor's hands," and later boiling it down to the five-word phrase "safety proceeds before the actor."

Spiro explained that this had to be true because "[t]he actor's job is to act," and thus when the gun is handed to him "his mind is somewhere else, in the being of another, a century away, an outlaw. He must be able to take that weapon and use it as the person he's acting would, to wave it, to point it, to pull the trigger like actors do in ways that would be lethal in the real world but are not lethal on a movie set."

Now, the case never made it to the jury to decide on a verdict because it was dismissed halfway through the trial after the judge ruled that the prosecution violated their disclosure obligations and Baldwin's due process rights. So we don't know whether jurors were persuaded by Spiro's argument, but the case is still a good example of a lawyer knowing the critical issue in their case and making a memorable point about it in their opening statement. Spiro's point sticks especially well because he reduces it to five simple yet direct words—"safety proceeds before the actor"—like a chef reducing a sauce to intensify its flavor. The lesson is that the simpler you can make your point, the more memorable it will be.

Remember, the goal is to make our take-home message clear and memorable. First, we need to have one. Some presentations fail here. It helps to pause and ask, "What is my ultimate message here?" "Do I have one?" Then ask, "Is it clear?" If not, rewrite it to make it concrete, actionable, and memorable.

This approach isn't limited to trial work. It can also be used for CLEs, client presentations, and written work.

I did this throughout writing this book. You'll notice that each chapter starts with a "rule," which is an actionable take-home message that captures the "gist" of everything in the chapter. I thought a lot about these. If I took a less concrete approach, I could have called Chapter 1 "Attention," Chapter 2 "Persuasion," and this chapter "Messaging," but those would have been less focused and less clear. I hope that by giving you actionable "rules," you might remember the gist of my advice and even a few details.

This is what the late law professor Irving Younger did in what is regarded as the most popular CLE of all time—*The Ten Commandments of Cross-Examination*. The title alone tells you what his message is and what the whole talk is about—do these ten things and you will be a better cross-examiner.

In the end, it pays to invest most of our time and thought into our take-home message. It might be the only thing our audience remembers.

Giving a Memorable Legal Presentation

I give a lot of continuing legal education (CLE) presentations. For each one, I work long and hard to find a memorable through line that ties the content together. Here are some I'm most proud of:

(1) Mastering Hearsay—When I teach the hearsay exceptions in the Evidence Code, I start by playing a 30-second clip from a 2016 NFL game between the Green Bay Packers and the Detroit Lions. Packers receiver Ty Montgomery is set to return a kickoff. The ball bounces to the 3-yard line near the sideline. Instead of fielding it there with Lions players sprinting towards him, Montgomery runs out of bounds and leans forward to grab the ball with his toes still out of bounds. As a result, Montgomery and the Packers get the ball at the 40-yard line. Why? Because the NFL rulebook says a loose ball is out of bounds when it touches *anything* that is outside the boundary line, including a player, and a kickoff out of bounds is generally advanced to the 40. The Packers scored on the drive and later won the game by a touchdown.[28]

After explaining this, I give the audience my through line: they need a "Montgomery Mindset" with the Evidence Code—meaning they need to know all the nuances—because it can mean the difference between winning and losing. The audience pays attention because they want to know how I am going to tie an NFL game to the Evidence Code (a knowledge gap). And then they remember the "Montgomery Mindset" because it is short, alliterative, and ties together the value of all the hearsay exceptions.

28. Rob Demovsky, *Stanford Smart: Ty Montgomery's Football IQ Shows Up for Packers*, ESPN (Sept. 27, 2016), https://www.espn.com/blog/green-bay-packers/post/_/id/33720/stanford-smart-ty-montgomerys-football-iq-shows-up-for-packers.

(2) The Secrets to Cross Examination—I follow a similar formula when I teach cross examination. I begin with a story about how UCLA basketball coach John Wooden would start each season making his players practice putting on their socks, without wrinkles or creases. Why? Because he believed wrinkles caused blisters, and blisters cost games. But he also wanted to teach a larger point—that small details were important, which led to his creed: "Details create success."[29]

This becomes my through line. Then I show how it can be applied to cross examination. For example, asking extremely short, one-fact questions helps control the witness because they don't invite long answers. Or how inflecting your voice downward at the end of a question can show your confidence in the suggested answer, signaling that the witness should not argue with you (play it in your head; imagine the following question with downward inflection at the end: "Mr. Jones, the light was red when you entered the intersection?").

(3) The Ethics of Witness Preparation—When I teach the ethics of witness preparation, my through line is "great witness prep *starts* with great ethics." The reason is that I want participants to see that knowing the ethical rules does more than just keep them out of trouble—it also leads to the best results. This is because when an attorney knows exactly where the ethical lines are, they can then use all the ethical prep tools available, walking right up to the line and leaving nothing on the table. I frame the lecture this way to appeal to everyone's desire not just to stay out of trouble, but also to win—a concept that doesn't usually come up in a lecture about ethics.

(4) Making Better Sentences—I give a legal writing lecture that focuses on improving the sentences attorneys write (making them shorter, avoiding nominalizations and prepositional phrases, etc.). At the beginning, I get the audience's buy-in by explaining why sentences matter—"because your sentences are the first way your reader will experience (and thus judge) your writing. Before they read the whole brief, before they read a section, and before they read a paragraph, they will read a sentence. Everything starts with a sentence." This becomes my through line and it captures the value of all the sentence-level lessons in the lecture.

29. Atul Gawande, *Personal Best*, New Yorker, Sept. 26, 2011.

The common theme running through these examples is that they all showcase the ultimate value of the material to the audience in a single sentence. And when the audience sees the value of what you're giving them in a legal presentation, the rule of self-interest says they are more likely to pay attention and remember it (see Chapter 2—"It's Not About You; It's About Them").

4

Rule Four: Make It Easy for Them

Let's keep going with our audience-centered approach.

By now, we've captured their attention. We're talking about stuff they care about. We've made our take-home message clear and designed our talk around it.

Now we're going to make sure everything else we say is easy for them to follow and process.

4.1 Avoid the Curse of Knowledge

All the lessons so far have encouraged us to think more about our audience and how everything is received from their perspective. This next lesson puts this mindset shift front and center.

The problem is one we've all seen—a presenter passionately discussing a subject they are a total expert in, yet the audience doesn't have a clue what they're saying. You'd think the presenter's passion and experience would be a recipe for success, but it's not. It's why they fail. The presenter has fallen victim to the "curse of knowledge."

The curse of knowledge occurs when a presenter knows so much about a topic that they can't remember what it was like when they didn't know anything.[1] Thus, they struggle to explain it clearly to newcomers. They use terms the audience doesn't understand, refer to concepts the audience never learned, and mention people and events the audience isn't familiar with. It is one of the biggest culprits of bad presentations.

It's not limited to public speaking. It applies to writing too. In writing, psychologist Stephen Pinker explains:

> It simply doesn't occur to the writer that her readers don't know what she knows—that they haven't mastered the argot of her guild, can't divine the missing steps that seem too obvious to mention, have no way to visualize a scene that to her is as clear as day. And so the writer doesn't bother to explain the jargon, or spell out the logic, or supply the necessary detail.[2]

We experience it in our daily lives too. Pinker gives two funny examples. First, he says it appears when he goes on the web to find a trusted-traveler program and has "to decide whether to click on GOES, Nexus, GlobalEntry, Sentri, Flux or FAST—bureaucratic terms that mean nothing to me."

He also sees it when he picks up a remote in his apartment but can't remember how to use it because of cryptic buttons that "may have to be held down for one, two or four seconds" and "sometimes two at a time." While the engineers who designed the remotes might have thought they were perfectly clear, Pinker did not.

This aligns with a famous quote by the playwright George Bernard Shaw: "The single biggest problem in communication is the illusion that it has taken place." We get so stuck in our own heads that we become oblivious to what is happening with our listeners.

Trial lawyers are especially vulnerable to this because we often spend years working up our cases before they get to trial. In that time, we become experts in the minutiae. We've reviewed hundreds if not thousands of documents. We've sat through lengthy depositions of key witnesses. We've worked hand in

---

1. *See* HEATH & HEATH, cited above in Chapter 1, note 17, at 19–20; McGOWAN, cited above in Chapter 1, note 6, at 265. It is also sometimes called the "expert blind spot." *See* AMBROSE ET AL., cited above in Chapter 2, note 1, at 99.

2. Steven Pinker, *The Source of Bad Writing: The "Curse of Knowledge" Leads Writers to Assume Their Readers Know Everything They Know*, WALL ST. J. (Sept. 25, 2014), https://stevenpinker.com/files/pinker/files/the_source_of_bad_writing_-_wsj_0.pdf.

hand with our experts, becoming so fluent in their field's jargon and acronyms that we probably deserve an honorary degree.

The problem can appear even in a simple DUI trial that an attorney may do early in their career at a local prosecutor or public defender's office. Go watch one and you might think everyone is talking in a foreign language when they start mentioning FSTs (field-sobriety tests), NHTSA (the National Highway Traffic Safety Administration), and HGN (horizontal gaze nystagmus).

Lawyers presenting CLEs or talking to clients become afflicted too. We've spent years in school and decades in practice becoming experts in our niche areas, learning arcane code sections, terminology, and precedents. And because we've attained this knowledge, we love talking to other experts about it and showing we are in the club. But we lose our ability to talk to less-experienced people.

How do we avoid the curse of knowledge?

It starts with recognizing the problem. When we prepare our presentation, ask if it will make sense to someone who knows nothing about our topic. Better yet, run it by a trusted friend, family member, or colleague and ask if it makes sense to them.[3]

Second, watch out for the curse's two biggest co-conspirators—jargon and acronyms. When we find them, replace them with plain language alternatives or define and explain them to the audience. This also makes us appear smarter—counterintuitive as that might be. Research from Columbia Business School shows that people who use complicated language often come across as less intelligent than people who don't.[4] So there is no reason for jargon.

Third, pay attention to our audience during our presentation. Are they meeting us with blank, empty stares? If so, step back and break things down for them. Remember what it was like when we knew nothing about this. Where did we start? That's a good place for them too.

The tips in the next few sections will also help.

3. *See* AMBROSE ET AL., cited above in Chapter 2, note 1, at 113.

4. Zachariah C. Brown, Eric M. Anicich & Adam D. Galinsky, *Compensatory Conspicuous Communication: Low Status Increases Jargon Use*, 161 ORGANIZATIONAL BEHAV. & HUM. DECISION PROCESSES 274 (2020); Derek Thompson, *Why Simple Is Smart*, THE ATLANTIC (Jan. 31, 2022), https://www.theatlantic.com/ideas/archive/2022/01/writing-tips-for-journalists-jargon-simplicity/621411/.

4.2 Tie It to What They Already Know

In the last 50 years, educational psychologists have uncovered a lot about how people learn. One thing most agree on is that people need to connect new information to things they already know to learn something new.[5]

One teaching guide says, "When students can connect what they are learning to accurate and relevant prior knowledge, they learn and retain more."[6] The prior knowledge gives the new information something to stick to.

It also helps when the presenter "activates" this prior knowledge because people aren't great at doing it themselves.

As lawyers, we have two easy ways to do this—analogies and metaphors. Both do the same thing. They compare the new information to something the audience already knows, which makes it easier for them to understand it. Using analogies also forces us to present new ideas in concrete—rather than abstract—language, which aids understanding too.

I've used analogies throughout this book. I told you to think about your audiences the same way big-wave surfers treat the ocean. I compared an audience's attention span during a talk to a campfire. I showed you tools to keep an audience's attention by discussing bingeworthy TV. I gave you a quote that referred to knowledge gaps as "mosquito bites on the brain." I said you should think of your through line as a "trump card in the jury room."

Analogies and metaphors are one of the best ways to simplify complex ideas, and great lawyers use them all the time. They are also effective antidotes to the curse of knowledge.

Let's look at some examples.

EXAMPLE 1: *ORACLE V. GOOGLE*

Intellectual property cases can be some of the most complicated cases lawyers handle. Thus, it's no surprise that the best IP lawyers rely on metaphors and analogies to explain hard concepts to their judges and juries.

A strong example comes from a billion-dollar copyright fight between Oracle and Google. Oracle sued Google for using Oracle's code in Goo-

5. AMBROSE ET AL., cited above in Chapter 2, note 1, at 15 ("there is widespread belief among researchers that students *must* connect new knowledge to previous knowledge in order to learn"); MAYER, cited above in Chapter 3, note 1, at 39.

6. *Id.*

gle's Android smartphones.[7] The code let programmers already familiar with the popular Java programming language work effectively with Android's platform by using commands they already knew from Java to create their new programs.

Google's defense turned on a critical distinction in copyright law: it argued the code portions it used couldn't be copyrighted because they represented an organizational system—an "idea" rather than creative expression—and ideas aren't protected by copyright. To help the court understand exactly how the code worked, Google needed an analogy.

Its lawyer, Robert Van Nest, chose something universally familiar—a file cabinet. On a later podcast, he revealed that his team tested various analogies with focus groups before trial. The file cabinet analogy proved the most effective and supported their central argument—that "no one has the right to the system of organization that everyone has been using for years."[8]

The analogy worked so well that Van Nest wheeled a physical file cabinet into the courtroom at trial. When Oracle's lawyers saw it gaining traction, they insisted that it be removed anytime a witness wasn't talking about it.[9] Ultimately, the analogy must have worked because the trial judge used a similar one in his ruling for Google—bookshelves in a library.[10]

Van Nest gives the following advice on using analogies in technology trials—you should aim for "something that is simple, something that is familiar to people, something that they are dealing with every day."[11] He also says "the analogy doesn't work unless you can use it a lot"—"you've got to use it in your opening, in your closing, and with your experts." In other words, give the audience a familiar lens through which to see everything new you give them.

---

7. *See Google LLC v. Oracle America, Inc.*, 593 U.S. 1 (2021).

8. *Unscripted Direct*, Episode 52, "The Billion Dollar File Cabinet (Analogies with Superstar Trial Lawyer Bob Van Nest)" (Sept. 27, 2022), https://www.unscripteddirect.com/#episodes.

9. *Id.* at 41:50.

10. Craig Anderson, *Google Lawyer Sticks to His Guns: Facing Long Odds, Robert Van Nest Wins Over Judge and Jury*, S.F. Daily J., June 6, 2012.

11. *Unscripted Direct*, cited above in note 8.

EXAMPLE 2: *SHELBY COUNTY V. HOLDER*

Some Supreme Court Justices write their opinions so they can be understood by everyday people. And to do so, they use analogies.

The late Justice Ruth Bader Ginsburg was a master at them. In a 2013 Voting Rights Act case, she used one that was so fitting it "went viral in the aftermath of the decision," appearing all over the media and internet.[12]

What did she say?

The case was *Shelby County, Alabama v. Holder*, 570 U.S. 529 (2013). In it, the majority threw out parts of the 1965 Voting Rights Act as unconstitutional. The sections at issue applied to only the parts of the country that had the longest history of voting discrimination. The sections subjected them to greater oversight whenever they wanted to change their election laws. As part of the majority's reasoning, it said that while the constraints made sense in the 1960s and 70s, they were no longer needed because the voting turnout gap in those states had significantly narrowed since the law was enacted.

Justice Ginsburg did not like this reason. She wanted to attack it in her dissent. She turned to an analogy.

She wrote that throwing out the regional protections of the Voting Rights Act when they were working was "like throwing away your umbrella in a rainstorm because you are not getting wet."[13]

This was a good response to the majority's logic, no matter what side you are on. Think about it. Saying that the protections aren't needed just because the problem has shrunk is not a great argument since it focuses on what the problem looks like with the protections in place. A better argument would also focus on what might happen if you removed them. And apparently, as Ginsburg noted, Congress had looked at "[v]olumes of evidence" when it reauthorized the legislation in 2006 that showed the prospects of backsliding in those states "was real."

Ginsburg's analogy resonated because it created a simple yet crisp image that anyone could understand. While it didn't change the Court's decision, it succinctly captured why the Act's supporters thought scrapping

12. Ellen D. Katz, Justice Ginsburg's Umbrella, in A NATION OF WIDENING OPPORTUNITIES? THE CIVIL RIGHTS ACT AT FIFTY 264 (Samuel R. Bagenstos & Ellen D. Katz eds., 2015).

13. *Shelby County, Alabama v. Holder*, 570 U.S. 529, 590 (2013) (Ginsburg, J., dissenting).

the provisions would be so harmful. And it drew public attention to what Ginsburg believed was a detrimental decision, which is the goal of any dissent. People who know very little about election laws could understand why she thought the decision was bad, and perhaps that could motivate them to seek change at the ballot box.

If nothing else, it is a good example of how something as simple as the rain and an umbrella can add weight to a legal argument.

EXAMPLE 3: DUI TRIALS

Let's look at one more. If you aren't familiar with DUI cases, the most common field sobriety test police officers perform is something called the "horizontal gaze nystagmus" (HGN) test.

In basic terms, the test has the suspect follow a pen with their eyes while the officer moves it back and forth. If the person's eyes "involuntarily jerk" when the officer does this, it suggests they've consumed alcohol, since studies show alcohol produces this distinct type of involuntary jerking in the eyes.

When a prosecutor gets to trial, it's tough to explain this to the jury in a way that makes sense. What's more, how are the jurors supposed to know that the officer saw this nystagmus when the jurors have never seen it themselves?

How about an analogy? Many experienced police officers will say the involuntary jerking looks like windshield wipers moving across a dry, dirty windshield. The wipers make it to the other side, but they jerk along the way. I bet you can see the image in your mind already.

With this established, the jury can understand what the officer is looking for, and how easy it is to spot. Jerking wipers on a dirty windshield look different than smooth wipers on a wet windshield. Now the jurors understand the new concept, almost instantly, thanks to activating their prior knowledge with an analogy.

Notice the similarities in the three analogies we looked at. They all have the same qualities Robert Van Nest aims for—they're simple, they're familiar, and they're things people deal with almost every day. They bring the audience up to speed and put them on the same page as the presenter. The curse of knowledge can't rear its ugly head here.

Use analogies and metaphors when you can. Finding the perfect one is part of the fun of being an advocate.

* * *

Beyond making things easier for our audience, activating their prior knowledge serves another goal. It makes the whole experience more interesting for them and boosts their attention. In other words, it helps us not be boring.

Philosopher and psychologist William James observed this at the turn of the last century. In a talk to teachers, he said:

> It is an odd circumstance that neither the old nor the new, by itself, is interesting: the absolutely old is insipid; the absolutely new makes no appeal at all. The old in the new is what claims the attention—the old with a slightly new turn.[14]

In *Hit Makers: The Science of Popularity in an Age of Distraction*, journalist Derek Thompson theorizes that this is why sequel movies dominate the box office. They offer viewers something that is both familiar and new. Thus, he says that the "best hit makers are gifted at creating moments of meaning by marrying new and old.... They are architects of familiar surprises."[15]

In *The Art of Advocacy*, Yale Law School lecturer Noah Messing gives another riff on this idea. He says that discussing familiar information before new information is "the cognitive equivalent of what happens to most people when they walk into a crowded room. If they immediately see a few friends, they will calm down." Thus, he recommends that lawyers can make their audiences more comfortable if they "greet them with a few old friends."

Courtrooms are unfamiliar places for many jurors, who are likely to feel intimidated and out of place when they walk in. But as soon as they hear lawyers talking about things they already know, with words they know, they feel more at home.

In short, presenting our message through what the audience already knows has many benefits. So do it.

---

14. William James, Talks to Teachers on Psychology (1899).

15. Derek Thompson, Hit Makers: The Science of Popularity in an Age of Distraction 7 (2017).

Quick Tip from an Advocate

Susan Har is Counsel at Hecker Fink LLP in Los Angeles. She is a highly accomplished trial lawyer and former federal prosecutor. I asked her for a tip about how to teach a jury complicated concepts with analogies. Here is what she said:

> I love using analogies with a jury, both because it helps simplify complicated concepts into something accessible and because it's an opportunity to empower the jury with confidence that they already know exactly how to approach the decision they are being asked to make. The key is to use an everyday analogy that comports with most common life experiences. While a juror might feel intimidated weighing in on a complicated fraud or embezzlement scheme, most jurors will feel far more confident in detecting when someone is acting deceptively or dishonestly—particularly if you draw an easy-to-understand analogy to a child's behavior when lying to their parents or covering their tracks out of guilt.
>
> Also, don't feel compelled to come up with an analogy that covers the entire case or mirrors all its facts. Most of the time, that's difficult to do and may result in an overly generic metaphor that can be flipped and used against you. You should feel free to pick an analogy to highlight just one key aspect of your case. Then, test it out on friends, family members, and anyone else who is willing to listen. They're the same type of audience as your jury and can give you valuable insight into whether an analogy will land or not.

4.3 Break It into Well-Paced, Bite-Sized Chunks

To learn new information, people need to process it in their working (short-term) memories, which have limited capacities.[16]

Most psychologists agree this is an active—not passive—process, meaning the learner must (1) sift through the information, (2) decide what's important, (3) decide how to organize it, and (4) compare and connect it to their existing knowledge.[17] Only when this process is finished can they learn the new thing.

To land our message, we need to break our presentation into bite-sized chunks and build in time for the audience to think about what we've said and reflect on it. If we instead assume their minds are empty vessels that we just need to pour information into, we've got it wrong.[18]

A better analogy is that we are serving a multi-course meal at a restaurant. They don't want all the courses at once. And they don't want it all shoved in their mouths. They want breaks and time to digest everything. In this way, our brains are like our stomachs. This is the same reason long-distance telephone numbers are broken into three sets of numbers. It's easier for the human brain to process and remember.

Teaching experts call this chunking. In their seminal guide to teaching higher education, husband and wife duo Richard Felder and Rebecca Brent tell us:

> Information fire-hosed at students nonstop is unlikely to make it to long-term memory and less likely to be subsequently retrieved and transferred. To increase the chances that your students will absorb important session content, give it to them in relatively small digestible chunks, followed by opportunities for them to retrieve and reflect on it and practice applying it.[19]

How can we incorporate this as lawyers?

First, we need to slow down and present at a good pace for our listeners. Trials and big presentations are exciting, adrenaline-fueled events. If we aren't careful, this adrenaline will drive us to talk too fast. Ask any court reporter

16. Mayer, cited above in Chapter 3, note 1, at 36.

17. *Id.* at 37–39; *see also* Richard M. Felder & Rebecca Brent, Teaching and Learning STEM: A Practical Guide 2, 112 (2016).

18. Mayer, cited above in Chapter 3, note 1, at 39.

19. Felder & Brent, cited above in note 17, at 72.

and they will tell you this is a problem for lawyers. Normal speaking rates range from 120 to 200 words per minute,[20] yet court reporters often see lawyers talking much faster than this.

Presentation experts say you should aim for 120 to 170 words per minute. Today, any smartphone can tell you how fast you are talking. If talking speed is an issue for you, practice with your phone and adjust as necessary.

Second, we need to check in with our audiences. In a CLE presentation, this is easy. We can periodically ask them, "How are we doing?" "Are you good here?" "Can we move on?" With juries, we aren't allowed to talk with them during opening statements and closing arguments, but most judges still allow the occasional check-in question that looks for nods (not verbal responses) from the jurors.

Thus, when you finish a topic, try asking the jurors, "Are we doing okay?" Or before you change slides, ask, "Can we keep going?" Most will give you a nod one way or the other, and you can use that information to adjust what you're doing. If they look worn out, you can recommend a stretch or bathroom break. Even if you don't ask questions, just looking out for discomfort and pained expressions can help.

Third, we need to design our talks in chunks. And at the end of each one, we need to cycle on the topic a bit to let the audience reflect on what we've said and signal to them that we're changing topics soon. It can be as simple as saying, "Okay, I've just talked about __________ and told you __________. Now I'm going to move on to the next thing." This also helps because at any given time, some of our audience will be checked out. These transitions tell them it is an easy time to check back in.

If you're presenting a story, like an opening statement at trial, think of your chunks as different chapters. John Hueston did this in the Enron trial.[21] Discussing his strategy, he says: "Chapter by chapter, the following theme was repeated for each defendant: lies on the outside, contrasted with true knowledge of Enron's financial state on the inside."

By doing so, he gave the jurors opportunities to follow and digest the storyline for each defendant. This shows that he, like most great trial lawyers, used an audience-centered approach. He made it easy for them.

---

20. Keith Rayner & Charles Clifton Jr., *Language Processing in Reading and Speech Perception Is Fast and Incremental: Implications for Event-Related Potential Research*, 80 Biol. Psychol. 4 (2009).

21. Hueston, cited above in Chapter 1, note 5.

4.4 Remove the Clutter

We help our audiences by removing the clutter from our presentations. By clutter, I mean anything that isn't essential to our message. Think unnecessary details and interesting but irrelevant tangents, back stories, and datapoints.

Clutter causes harm because it is extra information our listeners need to process with their already limited capacities. They might get the anecdote or be intrigued by the interesting yet unimportant statistic, but they'll miss our main message.

Psychologists call this clutter "extraneous information." In the words of Dr. Richard Mayer, "Extraneous material competes for cognitive resources in working memory and can divert attention from the important material, can disrupt the process of organizing the material, and can prime the learner to integrate the material with an inappropriate theme."[22]

He did 19 studies to test how extraneous information affects participants' learning. In 18 of them, learners did better with it excluded.[23]

In trials, facts get lawyers in trouble the most. Our cases are built around facts, and we love to show that we know all of them. The problem is many are irrelevant. In the words of legal writing teacher Gary Kinder, "Never confuse a fact with a relevant fact."[24]

Dates are big offenders. Many lawyers might be tempted to begin an opening statement with the following line: "On or about Wednesday, April 3, of 2022, the defendant. . . ." But often the fact it was a Wednesday doesn't matter. Neither does the exact date of April 3.

By including them, we put unnecessary strain on the audience's brains at the beginning of an opening. Since we mentioned them, the audience assumes they are important and will try to hold onto the information, making it compete with other important details in their limited headspace.

Locations are culprits too. Does it matter that the defendant was driving in the number 3 lane of the 10 freeway heading eastbound between Fairfax and La Brea? If it doesn't, why mention it? How about "the defendant was driving east on the 10 freeway?"

---

22. MAYER, cited above in Chapter 3, note 1, at 144.

23. *Id.*

24. *The 10 Myths of Legal Writing*, WORDRAKE, https://www.wordrake.com/writing-tips/the-10-myths-of-legal-writing.

And we can't forget job titles. Does it mean something that Ms. Jackson was the company's Senior Vice President of Strategic Initiatives for the Mid-Western Territory? Why not say she was the plaintiff's boss?

We do it in client and colleague presentations too. If we're giving a legal update about recent cases, usually the audience wants only the core facts and important holdings, not the entire backstory. But sometimes we feel compelled to include everything we know about the history of the case to show our expertise.

For example, earlier in this section, I talked about how *Shelby County v. Holder* ruled that parts of the 1965 Voting Rights Act were unconstitutional. I could have also added that when the Act was originally passed in 1965, it was intended to expire in five years, but in 1970 Congress renewed it for another five years, and then in 1975 for another seven years, and then in 1982 for another 25 years, and then in 2006 for another 25 years, taking us to today.

But none of that was relevant to the point I wanted to make about Justice Ginsburg's umbrella-in-the-rain analogy. So I omitted it. When it comes to your presentations, do the same.

This doesn't mean omit all details. Studies have shown that details that paint a vivid mental picture for the audience can boost a story's credibility and believability.[25] For example, in parole hearings, prisoners who apologize for their wrongs with detailed, concrete explanations are more likely to get parole than those who use more generic language.[26] Thus, details that support our legal arguments or give emotional weight to the story are extremely important.

Justice Sonia Sotomayor understood this early in her career when she was a New York prosecutor. When she tried jury cases, she would "elicit details with powerful sensory associations: the colors, the sounds, the smells, that lodge an image in the mind and put the listener in the burning house." In her words, "It is the particulars that make a story real."[27] And they are needed to "engage the jurors' empathy."

Another example of this is seen in the way great plaintiff's attorneys argue damages to a jury. In a case where someone is severely injured, or a wrongful

---

25. Jonathan Sadler & Melvin Manis, *Can the Availability Heuristic Explain Vividness Effects?*, 51 J. Personality & Soc. Psych. 26 (1986).

26. Jonah Berger, *The Magic of Knowing When to Use Concrete vs. Abstract Language*, Behavioral Scientist (2023), https://behavioralscientist.org/the-magic-of-knowing-when-to-use-concrete-vs-abstract-language/.

27. Sonia Sotomayor, My Beloved World 211 (2013). This example was also included in Patrick Barry, Good with Words: Writing and Editing 100 (2019).

death action where a family member is lost, it is possible to succinctly describe the harm or loss suffered, saying "Mr. Jones lost his leg" or "Susie Torres lost her father." But a skilled plaintiff's attorney would never limit their discussion of the harm to that. They would bring out all the details to show the jury what that loss means for their client and make the jury feel empathy. "That means Mr. Jones can no longer play in the Saturday-morning pickup basketball game he played in for the last 15 years with his high-school friends, which was his main way of maintaining those relationships that gave him so much fulfillment over the years." "Susie lost the person who drove her to all her swimming practices and knew everything she put into the sport. She's competing in the state finals for the first time this year and she can't imagine her dad not being there in the stands." Good plaintiff's attorneys bring out these details because they matter to the case and make the jury truly understand their client's experience.

My goal is not to give you conflicting advice about details that's hard to apply. A good practice with details is to ask yourself, does this add anything? Does my audience need it? Does it move the needle on a legal argument or help make my client's story feel more real? If the answer is no, cut it and make things easier for your audience.

The best attorneys are masters at selecting the right details to focus on and ignoring the rest. They let their best arguments shine, making persuasion happen faster and easier. As the painter Hans Hofmann once said, "Eliminate the unnecessary so that the necessary may speak."

EXAMPLE: JOHN HUESTON'S APPROACH TO THE ENRON TRIAL

John Hueston put these principles into practice in the Enron trial. In his essay about the trial, he explains that the hardest task in preparing the case was "deciding what will *not* be presented to the jury."[28]

In their years working up the case, his team discovered many fraudulent transactions at the company, but some were hard to tie to the two defendants—top executives Jeffrey Skilling and Ken Lay—and others required getting into complicated accounting rules. His team debated:

> [W]ould including such evidence, despite its complexity, provide useful 'atmospherics,' if not direct proof of the defendants'

28. Hueston, cited above in Chapter 1, note 5.

> fraud? If the jury were presented with episode after episode of misleading and fraudulent transactions, even with scant evidence of Lay or Skilling's involvement, might they conclude nonetheless that Lay and Skilling *must* have been knowingly involved?[29]

Hueston notes many attorneys would feel tempted to include this evidence, but his team opted not to. He writes, "A decision to include particular evidence for the sake of 'atmospherics' often reflects a failure to consider concretely what evidence will advance the determined trial narrative."[30]

Juries need "clear guideposts" from the attorney about what evidence truly matters. If attorneys include evidence just for their atmospherics, it presents a diffuse message and can lose the jury. Thus, Hueston says that a "winning approach" requires "clear and uncluttered themes" during all phases of trial.

The best trial attorneys think long and hard about this—and ruthlessly cut all but the most essential information.

Quick Tip from an Advocate

Mike Golden is the Director of Texas Law's Advocacy Program and practiced as a trial lawyer for 20 years. I asked him for a tip about editing down a presentation. Here is what he said:

> My very first mock trial coach moonlighted as a songwriter in Nashville. He relayed a lesson from one of his writing partners: "I became much more successful at crafting songs when I stopped trying to figure out what else I could put in them and started trying to see what else I could take out of them."
>
> A big mistake many lawyers make is thinking "if they [the jury, the judge] just knew everything that I know, they'd know why my side is the side of justice." But the more stuff you add into your argument, the less impact it has. This is commonly referred to as the "dilution effect," where critical information is lost in a sea of less-important data. It has also been called the "presenter's paradox": public speakers think

29. *Id.*
30. *Id.*

that if they keep adding information that favors them, it's like it's weighing the scales more and more in their favor, but the reality is that your audience isn't summing up your points, it's averaging them.

So, when you have two excellent points and four mediocre ones, your audience concludes that all of your points are each just so-so. When you write out or outline your argument, be over-inclusive when you start but edit vigorously, really trying to remove anything that's not necessary to make your point. Put an extra-critical eye on those points that you really love and try to objectively assess whether a neutral audience would find them necessary. I used to tell junior associates at my firm: before you send that email to the other side, find your favorite sentence and strongly consider deleting it.

Quick Tip from a Legal Recruiter

John O'Hara is the Chief Recruiting Officer at Gibson, Dunn & Crutcher LLP. I asked him for a speaking tip for candidates interviewing for law jobs. Here is what he said:

> Candidates interviewing for any position should make sure their statements are focused and clear. Rambling or meandering answers to interview questions can give the impression that the candidate isn't paying attention or isn't thoughtful. Overly complicated answers can dilute an otherwise positive or impactful response. It's worth thinking in advance about what messages someone wants to get across to their interviewer, whether about experience, skills, or why they're interested in the position, and practicing delivering those messages naturally but succinctly. That makes it easier to give direct answers that also highlight the candidate's selling points.

5

Rule Five: Prepare for Listeners, Not Readers

"A speech is not an essay on its hind legs."

This quote comes from James A. Winans, a Dartmouth public speaking professor in the early 1900s. He was one of the first modern public speaking teachers and he advocated for a conversational style instead of the pompous oratory that had been popular in the prior century. He cared deeply about the experience of listeners.

What Winans means in his quote is that when we prepare a speech for an audience, we need a different approach than when we write for a quiet reader. In other words, speech writing and essay writing are different—albeit related—crafts.

Public speaker John Coleman—an obvious disciple of Winans—tells us:

> Speeches and essays are of the same genus, but not the same species. Each necessitates its own craft and structure. If you're a great writer, don't assume it will translate immediately to the spoken word.[1]

1. John Coleman, *A Speech Is Not an Essay*, HARV. BUS. REV. (Sept. 11, 2014), https://hbr.org/2014/09/a-speech-is-not-an-essay.

Coleman also warns "those new to public speaking" that "the tendency to mimic the forms of writing we already know can be crippling."

Lawyers are especially prone to this because law school focuses more on legal writing than public speaking. Thus, when we start preparing a speech—be it an opening statement at trial, oral argument for the court, or legal presentation—we pull out a pen and paper, or open Microsoft Word, and start writing the same way we would a legal brief or memo.

We use full sentences. We use the same punctuation moves and sentence structures. We don't think twice about explanatory clauses, subordinate clauses, or introductory participle phrases. We follow all the popular legal writing maxims—"omit needless words," "drop intensifiers," don't get cute with attention grabbers.

And we think this is fine because when we read it quietly to ourselves, it makes sense in our heads. But the problem comes when someone can't see what we wrote and can only hear the words. Because the words were written for readers, not listeners, the listener has a harder time understanding them.

There are two reasons for this: (1) listeners can't see our punctation, and (2) listeners can't go back and revisit things they missed or didn't understand the first time.

For example, a parenthetical clause—like this one right here—might work well in a brief. But our listeners can't see the dashes. So lots of parenthetical clauses make the listener think we are rambling from one unrelated point to the next.

We need to prepare for listeners, not readers. How do we do this? The next few sections give some tips.

5.1 Use Even-Shorter, Even-Simpler Sentences

Our first strategy should be to use even-shorter, even-simpler sentences. This avoids the complex, awkward sentence structures that are especially hard for listeners to follow.

Let's look at some sentences that could work in a brief or memo but would be unnecessarily hard on a listener.

EXAMPLE 1: THE LONG EXPLANATORY CLAUSE

> Plaintiff, **who had never received a poor performance review in her entire 25-year career**, got her first one shortly after reporting Karl's misconduct.

Because our listener can't see the commas that signal the explanatory clause in bold, they have no idea where the sentence is going. They need to hold all 23 words in their working memories until the sentence is finished to make sense of it.

A better rewrite for listeners would be:

> Plaintiff had never received a poor performance review in her entire 25-year career. But she got one shortly after reporting Karl's misconduct.

EXAMPLE 2: SUBORDINATE CLAUSES

> **Because it was raining hard and John did not have an umbrella, and since traffic looked clear**, he darted across the street.

Again, the listener can't see the commas. Thus, they are required to hold not just one, but two long-subordinate clauses in their working memory before they know where it's going.

A better rewrite would be:

> It was raining hard, and John did not have an umbrella. Because traffic looked clear, he darted across the street.

Some would say this rewrite is also better for readers, and that's probably true. But the point is that the first version *could* work for a reader. It would be very hard on a listener.

EXAMPLE 3: THE LONG INTRODUCTORY CLAUSE

This example comes from the closing argument by one of Amber Heard's attorneys in her case with Johnny Depp. Here is how he began the closing:

> **In trying to convince you that Mr. Depp has carried his burden of proof in proving that he was never abusive to Amber on even one occasion**, think about the message that Mr. Depp and his attorneys are sending to Amber and by extension to

> every victim of domestic abuse everywhere. If you didn't take pictures, it didn't happen. . . .[2]

His first sentence is 51 words long. More than half those words (27) appear in the long introductory clause in bold. In public speaking, most of your sentences should be 20 words or fewer. Thus, this long sentence with the long windup doesn't work for listeners. It packs too much information into one sentence.

A better rewrite would break each point into its own sentence. For example:

> Mr. Depp has the burden of proof in this case. He needs to prove he was never abusive to Amber—not even once. But what message does he try to send with his argument? He wants to tell Amber and domestic abuse victims everywhere that if you didn't take pictures, it didn't happen. But remember, members of the jury, it is his burden to prove he *wasn't* abusive. It's not Amber's burden to prove he was.

EXAMPLE 4: PARTICIPLE PHRASES

> **Terrified she wouldn't make payroll that month**, Rachel took out a bridge loan.

This is another awkward phrase for listeners. It starts with a long participle phrase that will eventually modify "Rachel," but the listener doesn't know that until the sentence is over. The listener also doesn't know who the subject is (Rachel) until more than halfway through the sentence.

This is true for the reader too, but they can process around 300 words per minute, compared to the listener's average of 150 words. People's visual memories are also superior to their auditory memories.[3] Thus, the wait is less taxing for the reader, and seeing the comma helps them immediately comprehend the sentence's structure.

A better rewrite for listeners would be:

> Rachel was terrified she wouldn't make payroll that month. So she took out a bridge loan.

---

2. *Depp v. Heard*, closing argument, May 27, 2022, available at https://www.youtube.com/watch?v=e2rFxMe2PN4

3. Coleman, cited above in note 1.

Good legal writing calls for short, simple sentences.[4] But good public speaking calls for even-shorter, even-simpler sentences. Shorter planned sentences also make it easier to ditch our notes, which we should always do.

In *The Articulate Advocate*, trial advocacy instructors Brian Johnson and Marsha Hunter recommend that presenters "speak in phrases, not whole sentences."[5] This is good advice. The only way listeners can tell a speaker is punctuating their thoughts is when the speaker either pauses or changes their intonation or both.

Speaking in phrases, not sentences, reminds us to do these things. And it helps us present our ideas in shorter chunks that are easier for listeners to follow.

5.2 Be More Repetitive and Less Subtle

Unlike readers, listeners can't go back and reread anything they missed or didn't grasp the first time. We should also assume that at least 20 percent of our audience is tuned out at any given time. So what might be boring and needless repetition in a brief can be essential for listeners to understand what is happening.

We need to repeat and review our key points a few times to make sure everyone hears and understands them. (A "few" still means a small number—two or three at most; too much repetition is a big juror pet peeve.) We don't think about this when writing a brief or memo. If we approach speech writing with a legal-writing mindset, we won't create something that is optimally suited for how people actually listen.

It also helps to highlight and announce our key points before stating them. Here is an example: "Members of the jury, here is the point, and it's really important. I want this to stick with you...."

When you start doing this, you will notice heads lifting in the audience. This is because even when an audience member is thinking about something else, they are subconsciously listening for cues that they should bring their attention back to the presentation. They are also aware of other people in the

4. *See* BRIAN A. GARNER, LEGAL WRITING IN PLAIN ENGLISH §§ 6–7 (2d ed. 2013).

5. BRIAN K. JOHNSON & MARSHA HUNTER, THE ARTICULATE ADVOCATE: NEW TECHNIQUES OF PERSUASION FOR TRIAL LAWYERS 97 (2009).

audience. If your signaling makes their neighbor perk up, they will feel the social pressure to perk up as well.

Notice also that I used an intensifier in my example, saying the point was "really important." These intensifiers are often signs of less-elegant writing, but they highlight extra important information for listeners. Thus, it's not as important to strictly follow the legal writing advice about dropping all intensifiers. Don't go overboard with them because they lose their effectiveness the more you use them. Remember, you can only have a few "really important" points. But they aren't as evil in public speaking.

All this is to say, be less subtle. Good legal writing aims for elegant conciseness. But given the nature and habits of our listeners, speakers can't afford the same subtlety. We need to prepare for listeners, not readers.

5.3 Plan the Whole Performance, Not Just the Words

When preparing our speeches, we can plan things like hand gestures, vocal emphasis, changes in pace and volume, movements around the room, visuals, and so on. We can also appeal to our audience's auditory senses. We can get the full benefit from words that rhyme, alliterations that sound good, and words that please the ear. If we see the task as simply one of writing, we forget these tools, which are some of the best ways to inject style and emotion into a speech.

Thus, I do not recommend spending your entire speech-crafting time at the desk or a computer. You should spend at least half your time away from it, and you should think about your rehearsals as a key part of the writing process.

Stand up and say your thoughts out loud. How do they sound? Are the words you chose hard and awkward to say? Can you choose different words that are easier and sound better to the ear?

Does your written sentence sound too formal when you say it out loud? Does it give you places to breathe? Can you rework it to make it conversational?

Can you use a hand gesture to help punctuate an idea and make it clearer? For example, if you are listing three pieces of evidence that support an argument, would it help to hold up one, two, and three fingers as you go through them?

What facial expression will you make and what tone of voice will you use when discussing the opponent's arguments?

When you want to transition to a new chapter, can you walk to a new part of the room to signal this?

When you reach one of your biggest points, how long will you pause to let it sink in? Is there a good visual you can put up at the same time?

All these things are easier to think about and plan when we get out of our chair and focus on the whole performance, not just the words.

We talked about some of the advantages writers have over speakers—readers can see writers' punctuation, process writers' words faster, and have bigger visual memories. But speakers have some advantages too. We should prepare to our strengths, not weaknesses.

Writers need to rely on their words alone to evoke emotion. Speakers can do it with their voice, body language, pictures, videos, and moments of silence. Speakers can see their audience and connect with them in real time.

Much of this can and should be planned. The next few chapters discuss how to do it.

Quick Tip from an Advocate

Jonathan Davidi is a trial attorney at Panish | Shea | Ravipudi LLP in Los Angeles, where he represents individuals in personal injury, wrongful death, and product defect cases. He has obtained over $200 million in verdicts and settlements for his clients. I asked him for a tip about how he plans to keep the jury engaged. This is what he said:

> You have to plan your "power pauses." These are different from normal pauses where you might be transitioning topics or remembering what to say next. Figure out where you want the jury to give you extra focus, and plan to use that opportunity to pause—either right before or right after your statement. Trial lawyers often think that keeping a jury's attention requires continually speaking and moving to the next point before the jurors get bored. In reality, the moment you *stop* speaking is when their ears perk up even more, allowing you to deliver a point with more impact.

6

Rule Six: Give Them Something Good to Look At

Slides can elevate a presentation or make it feel like torture. At their worst, they cause "death by PowerPoint," a condition where the audience starts to contort themselves in their chairs—looking at their phones, the clock, the door, anything to ease their pain—until they finally turn into zombies ready to eat you.

We've all suffered through these presentations, and we know PowerPoint causes them. So the first question is, should we use slides at all?

For all but extremely short presentations, the answer is yes.

The reason is that people learn better from words *and* images than words alone. Visuals done well make our presentation the best it can be. It might be okay without them, but it is better with them. This is why this chapter is called "give them something *good* to look at."

We owe much of what we know about this to Dr. Richard Mayer, an educational psychologist at the University of California, Santa Barbara. He is the country's leading expert on "multimedia learning," which just means learning from words and images.

Dr. Mayer spent his career obsessed with one question—"Do people learn better from words and images than just words alone?" Over 35 years, he conducted more than a dozen studies to test this. All of them showed the answer was "yes."[1] People learn better with images involved.

Some lawyers have caught on. In 2006, Texas trial lawyer Mark Lanier gave a PowerPoint opening statement that was so compelling it made the news. The headline in the *L.A. Times* was "Making a (Power)Point of Not Being Tiresome."[2]

The article called the 253-slide presentation "mold-breaking" and "the opposite of boring." "Jurors apparently agreed: They awarded the plaintiff's family $253 million, coincidentally $1 million per slide."[3]

So the real question is how do we do visuals well? How do we create million-dollar slides?

That's what the rest of this chapter is about.

6.1 Use Mostly Pictures and Limit the Words, Seriously

By now, most people have heard the advice that we should use lots of pictures, keep slides simple, and not read them like a teleprompter. Yet people still violate it every day. This is strange because these same people generally agree with the advice. They just don't think it applies to them.

So let me say it a different way. This advice is not some lofty ideal we should aspire to. It is a matter of life and death for our presentation.

I'm not being overly dramatic. It really is.

Very smart people have done the research, and it shows the more words we put on a slide, the less the audience will absorb and remember.[4] This is because our brains are much better at processing pictures than text.

---

1. MAYER, cited above in Chapter 3, note 1, at 117.

2. Claire Hoffman, *Making a (Power)Point of Not Being Tiresome*, L.A. TIMES (Apr. 19, 2006), https://www.latimes.com/archives/la-xpm-2006-apr-19-fi-powerpoint19-story.html.

3. *Id.*

4. FELDER & BRENT, cited above in Chapter 4, note 17, at 79–80; MAYER, cited above in Chapter 3, note 1, at 281.

The more text we show, the greater the chance we will give our audience cognitive overload.[5] As brain scientist John Medina says, "Reading creates a bottleneck" for our mind.[6] Too much of it causes the brain to shut down, especially when it is trying to process competing information like spoken words.

On the other hand, because our brains are so good at processing pictures, pictures perfectly complement an oral presentation. One study showed that adding pictures to a presentation boosted the audience's memory of it three days later by 65 percent.[7]

Dr. Medina says, "Put simply, the more visual the input becomes, the more likely it is to be recognized—and recalled."[8]

This doesn't mean all text is bad. Research shows that slides with a clear headline at the top, succinctly stating our most important point, improve the audience's comprehension and retention.[9]

To have this effect, the headline needs to actually state our point. It should not be a vague reference to our topic. For example, a headline that says "defendant's DNA was the only DNA on the murder weapon," is better than one that says "evidence of defendant's guilt."

In short, the best slides follow a specific formula:

a visual image + a brief headline with the main point[10]

Coincidentally, this is the formula Mark Lanier used for his million-dollar slides in that 2006 opening that made the news.[11] His visual-aid consultant, Cliff Atkinson, published an excellent book called *Beyond Bullet Points* that discusses their strategy in detail. But most of it boiled down to having just one idea per slide, with a simple headline illustrated by a simple graphic.

Following this formula means we may end up with more slides than we otherwise would have. This is a good thing. Fearing death by PowerPoint, some people believe they need fewer slides, but they are wrong. They need *simpler* slides.

---

5. Medina, cited above in Chapter 1, note 13, at 233–234.

6. *Id.* at 234.

7. *Id.*

8. Medina, cited above in Chapter 1, note 13, at 233.

9. Joanna Garner & Michael Alley, *How the Design of Presentation Slides Affects Audience Comprehension: A Case for the Assertion-Evidence Approach*, 29 Int'l J. Eng'g Educ. 1564 (2013); Mayer, cited above in Chapter 3, note 1, at 166, 207.

10. Felder & Brent, cited above in Chapter 4, note 17, at 80.

11. Cliff Atkinson, Beyond Bullet Points 14–15 (4th ed. 2018).

Figure 3: PowerPoint's Animations Feature

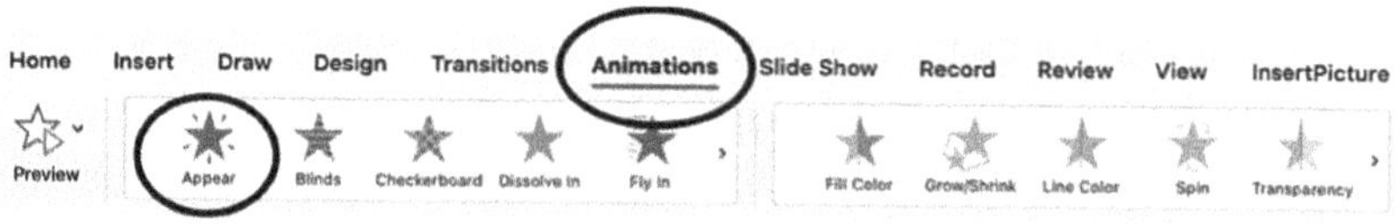

Having more, simpler slides also keeps the audience engaged because it gives them new visual stimuli more often. If you remember Chapter 1.3, bringing more change into the courtroom is a good thing.

This method also helps us break our presentation into digestible chunks. The "chunking" principle we discussed in Chapter 4.3 applies equally to the multimedia part of our presentation. Dr. Mayer's studies have shown this too.[12] This means our slides should focus on one idea at a time.

We can do this by putting different ideas on different slides, or using PowerPoint's "animation" feature, which lets us present slides slowly by introducing our text and images piece by piece. But if you use the animation feature, don't choose the crazy ones that have your words and pictures flying into the page from all angles. The simple "appear" animation works best (shown in Figure 3).

Limiting the text on our slides also stops us reading them like a teleprompter. So it's a foolproof recipe for success.

* * *

Trust the research. Use lots of pictures (or videos) and limit the text.

If you don't have pictures, go get them. Even if the events in your trial weren't captured in pictures or videos, you can still take pictures and videos of the scene. And it is easy to get pictures of the witnesses from social media, deposition videos, and company websites.

Put these pictures up when telling your story. Take the jurors to the scene with your visuals. All the research says this will make them more engaged and remember better.

Visuals also guarantee your jurors will have the same mental picture. Your job in trial is to get all of them—or, depending on the case and venue, most of them—to agree on what happened. It helps if they start by having the same mental image of where it took place, who was involved, and what they looked

12. Mayer, cited above in Chapter 3, note 1, at 247.

Figure 4: George Floyd Opening Timeline

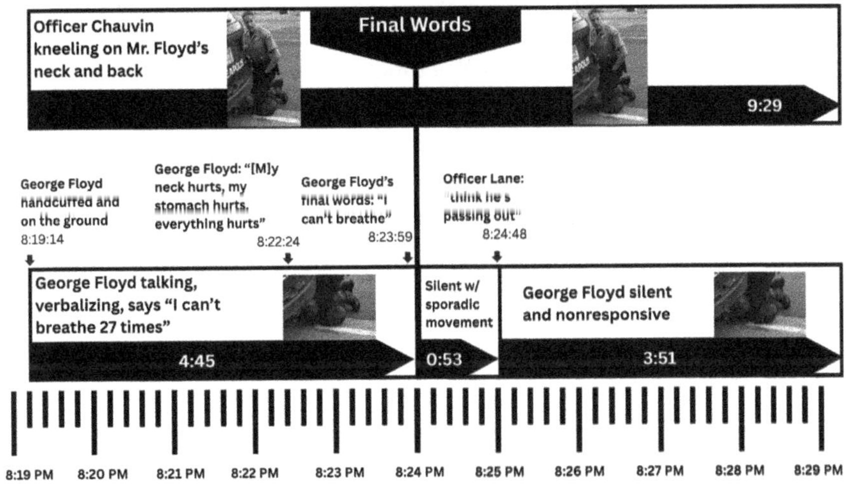

like. On the other hand, if they are all playing different movies in their heads based on just what the witnesses said, good luck!

Diagrams, timelines, graphs, maps, and relationship charts work too. Broadly speaking, each of these falls into a category of visuals called "concept maps"—a term used by educators.[13] A concept map is a visual that shows the relationship between pieces of information. They work because they help the viewer organize the information in their minds and see the big picture better than verbal narration can.

Timelines are a terrific example. They are far better at helping someone put multiple events in temporal context than verbal narration is because they don't require the person to keep track of the order of events in their working memories. Instead, it's all there for them on the timeline.

For example, look at the timeline prosecutor Jerry Blackwell used in his opening statement in the George Floyd murder trial (see Figure 4).

This timeline shows everything that happened during the 9 minutes and 29 seconds that Officer Chauvin was kneeling on Floyd's neck. It shows Floyd said "I can't breathe" 27 times. It shows he said his last words at 4 minutes and 45 seconds. And it shows he laid silent and non-responsive for another 3 minutes and 51 seconds, while Chauvin stayed in the same position.

13. Felder & Brent, cited above in Chapter 4, note 17, at 80.

This information has more impact when we see it plotted on a visual timeline. Blackwell's timeline is also great because it uses no more words than necessary and incorporates pictures.

Watch Blackwell's opening on YouTube and you will also see that he introduced the elements of this slide one at a time. He didn't force his audience to digest the whole thing at once—just the specific idea he focused on in the moment. By the end, he left the jury with a powerful and lasting visual that they saw him build in real time, brick by brick.

* * *

Concept maps are effective even when they contain mostly words, because they still give the audience a visual way to organize the information.

For example, a concept that comes up in domestic violence cases is the "cycle of abuse." The cycle of abuse is a tragic pattern that features in many domestic-violence relationships, especially when the abuser has psychological power or control over the victim.[14]

It usually involves four distinct phases that repeat: (1) a tension building phase, (2) the abusive incident, (3) a honeymoon or reconciliation phase, and (4) a calm phase. It is often used to answer why the victim doesn't leave the relationship, or why they might minimize the conduct when they talk about it later.

Since it follows a cyclical pattern, it is a perfect concept to illustrate visually instead of orally. See Figure 5 for an example.

Most textbooks, articles, and presentations discussing the cycle of violence use this visual. Many prosecutors in domestic violence cases use it too. It is a terrific example of an effective concept map. It includes mostly words, but it is simple and easy to process, and it illustrates the cyclical nature of the pattern better than any verbal description could.

Similarly, prosecutors in racketeering cases use organization charts to show the members and hierarchies in a criminal organization. These are concept maps too, and they are better at quickly illustrating the relationships people share than trying to describe the relationships in words. Figure 6 gives an example of what one might look like.

In short, some concepts are easier to show visually than with spoken words. In your next trial or presentation, look out for them. They present a great

---

14. *See* LENORE WALKER, THE BATTERED WOMAN (1980).

Figure 5: The Cycle of Abuse

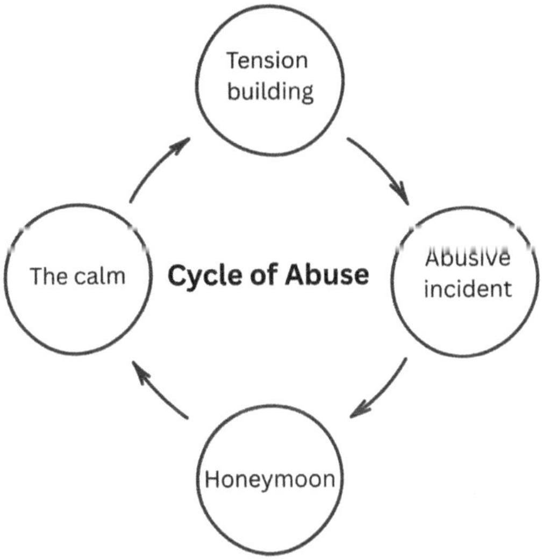

Figure 6: Crime Organization Chart

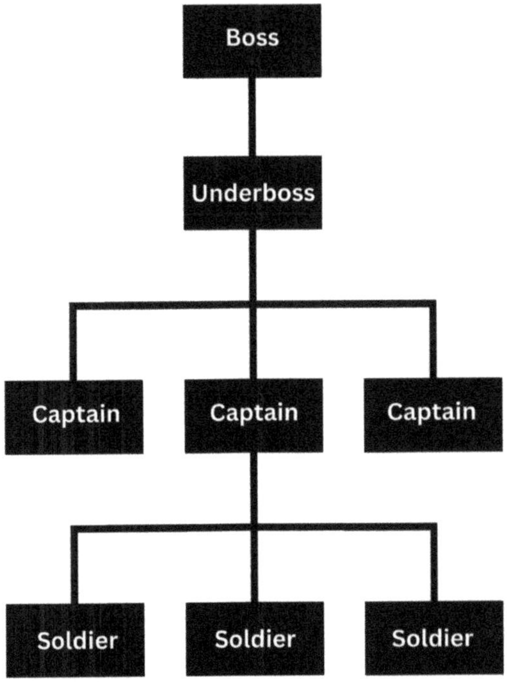

opportunity to create visuals to bring an extra dimension to your talk. Just remember, the more visual your image is, the easier it is for your audience to quickly get it and remember it. Slides with bullet points or lists of information are not great visuals. Instead, make slides that give the audience a helpful way to organize information in their minds.

* * *

I hear two excuses from people who insist on filling their slides with text:

1. It's easier for them to have everything they plan to say on the slides, and it will ensure they don't forget anything; and
2. They understand the advice, but they want to make sure the audience has all the information in writing, so they don't need to take notes and can take it home.

The irony is that overloading the slides with text defeats both goals.

While putting everything on the slides may seem easier for the speaker in the moment, it makes the whole presentation harder for them. It makes it harder for them to hold the audience's attention and connect with them, which is the whole reason the speaker is there.

Remember, the slides aren't for us; the slides are for them. *Everything* is for them. If we spend most of our time reading the slides, we ruin any chance of connecting with our audience. Even if we don't read the slides, some members of our audience will. That too will ruin our chance of connecting with them.

Second, by giving the audience all the information on the slides, we've shrunk the chance they will get anything from us or our talk. We've minimized our importance. And we've designed it so they will be so overloaded with information flying at them that they won't know what to focus on, won't be able to keep track of it, and their brains will shut down. They will be ecstatic when it is over, assuming they didn't sneak out before then. And the whole experience will have been so uninspiring that they will throw our slide handouts in the trash.

Don't think of your slides as a handout. If you want to give them a handout with information to take home, great. Do that. But don't put it all on the screen to distract them while they're there to pay attention to you.

In the end, use mostly pictures and less text. It's a matter of life or death.

6.2 Don't Read the Slides— I Repeat, Don't Read the Slides

Don't read the slides.

This is another piece of advice most people have heard, but for some reason don't follow. It's usually for selfish reasons—the slides are an easy crutch. If the presenter puts everything they plan to say on the slides and just shows up and reads them, they can shave hours off their prep time. And they don't have to stress about remembering anything.

Another reason is more innocent. People have heard that there are two learning styles in every audience—visual and auditory. Thus, they think that they can appeal to both styles by putting text on their slides and reading it to the audience. The visual folks will read it themselves; the auditory folks will listen.

The problem is the learning-style thing is a myth. While people may think that they have certain learning styles, studies show that teaching to someone's self-reported learning style does not result in better learning.[15]

More importantly, studies show that almost *everyone*[16] does worse when long written passages are shown and read to them at the same time.[17] Dr. Mayer attributes this to cognitive overload, and he says it is created by forcing people to compare the incoming streams of printed and spoken text.[18]

When we present people with written and spoken text at the same time, they try to process all of it. They try to process the written words through their visual channel and the spoken words through their auditory channel. Then they try to compare the two streams to make sure they are consistent.

But the problem is these channels run at different speeds. The average adult can read 300 words a minute but only follow speech closely at around 160 words per minute. Thus, when the same information is presented to both channels, the visual channel constantly gets ahead of the auditory channel and that frustrates the learner who is trying to compare the streams of information.

---

15. Stephanie Alley et al., *Does Matching a Personally Tailored Physical Activity Intervention to Participants' Learning Style Improve Intervention Effectiveness and Engagement?*, 28 J. Health Psych. 889 (2023); *see also* Olga Khazan, *The Myth of 'Learning Styles,'* The Atlantic (Apr. 11, 2018), https://www.theatlantic.com/science/archive/2018/04/the-myth-of-learning-styles/557687/; Mayer, cited above in Chapter 3, note 1, at 192.

16. People with visual and hearing impairments are an exception. If they are in our audience, we should accommodate them.

17. Mayer, cited above in Chapter 3, note 1, at 186.

18. *Id.*

It's like being in stop-and-go traffic. Or dragging a slow toddler when walking. Dr. Mayer explains that putting people in this situation forces them to use cognitive resources to run this comparison that they could otherwise use to just process the information.[19] So in a presentation, learning is more efficient when our words are presented in spoken form alone, not printed form.[20]

If you are like me, you've experienced this firsthand. When forced to sit through these types of presentations, I get a headache when the speaker reads a long passage that they have also put on the screen. So Dr. Mayer's explanation makes sense to me.

Again, the research tells us that reading a bunch of text from slides is not good for our audience. And since it's all about the audience, we shouldn't do it. It doesn't matter how much time we can save preparing, or how much stress we can alleviate by not having to remember our content. All that matters is the experience we give our listeners.

6.3 Ditch the Bells and Whistles; Instead, Focus on Backgrounds, Colors, and Fonts That Make It Easy to Read

When it comes to tedious PowerPoint presentations, we don't deserve all the blame. Microsoft deserves some too.

This is because PowerPoint comes loaded with fancy bells and whistles that interfere with communicating our core message. I'm talking about the default templates and backgrounds that make our presentations look like high-end marketing documents; the impressive animations that make us look like tech wizards; and the endless stock-image options that make us look like every other presenter in town, fake and unoriginal.

We are tempted to use these because everyone else does. And we think it is part of looking "professional." But the research shows it hinders our message.[21]

The reason should be familiar by now. This is all extra clutter—Dr. Mayer calls it "extraneous information"—that competes for our audience's limited

19. Mayer, cited above in Chapter 3, note 1, at 192.

20. *Id.* at 202.

21. Mayer, cited above in Chapter 3, note 1, at 143.

Figure 7: Intricate PowerPoint Background

cognitive resources and distracts from our core message. Remember, everything we add to a slide the audience needs to process.

Think the intricate background in Figure 7 takes your slides to the next level? Think again.

In 18 of 19 tests, Dr. Mayer found that learners who got concise presentations did better than those who got presentations with interesting but irrelevant stuff added.[22]

So how should we design our presentations? With our audience in mind. The slides should be simple and easy for them to process.

No one ever went wrong with a solid background. In fact, that's what I recommend.

Our color choice should depend on the room, the lighting, and the screen we're presenting on. If we're presenting on an LCD screen that emits its own light, we have the most options because most colors show up well on them. Still, darker backgrounds are easier on the eyes, so I'd choose one of them all else being equal (black, dark blue, dark gray, etc.).

If we're in a well-lit room and using a projector, a lighter background will probably show up better. The easiest way to determine what's best is to learn about the room and test it out.

---

22. Mayer, cited above in Chapter 3, note 1, at 143.

Once we've chosen our background, our text colors should be ones that provide the most contrast and, thus, readability. Light text on a dark background; dark text on a light background. Simple as that.

Our fonts should also be ones that people can read easily from far away. These are fonts with clean lines, well-balanced letters, and good spacing. Fonts designed for headlines and billboards are the best options. I use Helvetica and Palatino the most. Helvetica is a famously readable font with tall letters.[23] It is used widely by governments for everything from income tax forms to signs at train stations and airports. Palatino has large proportions and was designed for headings, advertisements, and display printing.[24] It also appears well even on poor-quality paper, and it is easy to read at a distance or in small sizes.

If you want to know a font's original purpose, look it up online. And if you really want to geek out, you can watch a whole 80-minute documentary about Helvetica called—wait for it—"Helvetica" (2007).

Another decision with fonts is whether to use serif or sans-serif fonts. Serif fonts (like Palatino) have small decorative strokes at the ends of some letters—like the little feet at the bottom of this capital "A" and "H." Sans serif fonts (like Helvetica) do not. Their letters have clean lines. Here is how the same letters look in Helvetica: "H" and "A."

Some people believe different fonts connote different levels of credibility and persuasiveness, although there isn't much hard science behind it. Generally, they say that serif fonts are more persuasive, likely because they are associated with credible sources like textbooks and newspapers, while sans serif fonts are used more in advertising. The United States Supreme Court uses a serif font (Century Schoolbook).

In 2012, writer and director Errol Morris ran a quiz in *The New York Times* that gives some support for this.[25] The quiz had about 45,000 participants read an essay that was shown in one of six randomly assigned fonts. They were then asked whether they believed the claims in the essay. The results showed that the participants presented with the three serif fonts (Baskerville, Computer Modern, and Georgia) agreed with the claims more than the participants

---

23. "Helvetica." *Wikipedia*, Wikimedia Foundation, https://en.wikipedia.org/wiki/Helvetica.

24. "Palatino." *Wikipedia*, Wikimedia Foundation, https://en.wikipedia.org/wiki/Palatino.

25. Earl Morris, *Are You an Optimist or a Pessimist?*, N.Y. Times (July 9, 2012), https://archive.nytimes.com/opinionator.blogs.nytimes.com/2012/07/09/are-you-an-optimist-or-a-pessimist/.

presented with the other three fonts (Trebuchet, Helvetica, and Comic Sans). Comic Sans did the worst.

Does this mean we should use serif fonts when we are trying to persuade? Not exactly. But it won't hurt us, as long as the choice is easily readable. We should also stay far away from Comic Sans.

In the end, we will be the most persuasive if we've captured our audience's attention, made it about them, and designed it to fit how they absorb and learn information. With visuals, that means simple, easy-to-process slides that contain mostly pictures.

Quick Tip from an Advocate

Matt Cave is a founding partner of Kibler Fowler & Cave LLP—a litigation and trial boutique in Los Angeles. He has litigated high-stakes disputes all over the country and has tried cases in both state and federal court. I asked him for a tip about using visuals at trial. This is what he said:

> I always use a few demonstratives at trial, especially with a jury. Our team spends a lot of time on the demonstratives because they can have a major impact.
>
> For example, at a recent jury trial, we argued that our defendant-client, a landlord, offered a "reasonable accommodation" to a disabled tenant by offering a reserved parking space around the corner from his unit. The plaintiff disputed the reasonableness of the accommodation and instead demanded a reserved parking space directly in front of his unit.
>
> But the plaintiff did not dispute that he regularly walked to the community pool, which was farther away from his unit than the offered parking space. Rather than just tell this to the jury, I pulled out a scaled map of the community and had a defense witness draw a line from the plaintiff's unit to the pool and then another line from the plaintiff's unit to the offered parking space.
>
> The jury saw that the line to the pool was quite a bit longer, which put a lie to the plaintiff's testimony about how

difficult it would have been for him to walk to the offered parking space. And it was more powerful for the jury to draw its own inferences based on my 30-second visual presentation than to have our witness testify about what the jury should have concluded.

7

Rule Seven: Bring Your Best Voice

You've probably heard someone say that "it's not what you say but how you say it."

Maybe they even gave you statistics. Like only 7 percent of your message is communicated by your words, but 38 percent is communicated by your tone of voice and 55 percent by your body language.

This is misinformation. And it is crazy how many communications "experts" perpetuate it.

The "7-38-55" myth traces back to misinterpreted research by UCLA psychologist Albert Mehrabian from 1967.[1] The research had nothing to do with people giving speeches. Instead, it looked at how subjects interpreted another person's one-word statements about their own emotions, especially when the person's non-verbal behavior conflicted with the statement.

In one study subjects listened to recordings of single words, like "thanks" and "terrible," pronounced in positive, neutral, and negative tones. When the

1. Albert Mehrabian & Susan R. Ferris, *Inference of Attitudes from Nonverbal Communication in Two Channels*, 31 J. Consulting Psychol. 248 (1967); Albert Mehrabian & Morton Wiener, *Decoding of Inconsistent Communications*, 6 J. Personality & Soc. Psychol. 109 (1967).

subjects were asked to guess what emotion the speaker was conveying, they were more influenced by the tone of voice than by the words themselves.

Across two papers with 137 subjects, Mehrabian generalized that listeners in these situations focus 7 percent on the words, 38 percent on the tone, and 55 percent on the body language/facial expressions.

This shouldn't come as a surprise. Anyone whose spouse has told them "I'm fine" in a negative tone with their arms crossed and a frowned face knows that their spouse is not, in fact, "fine."

But this doesn't mean that when we tell a ten-minute story or give a long legal presentation the audience is getting 93 percent of the meaning from our tone of voice and facial expressions. Mehrabian himself says that is "absurd."[2]

In a 2019 interview, Mehrabian said his "findings have been overgeneralized over the decades." His studies dealt specifically with the role of nonverbal behavior in communicating one's emotions, feelings, and attitudes. Unless a communicator is talking about their own emotions, feelings, or attitudes, the research doesn't apply.[3]

It also does not apply when a communicator says a lot more than just one word—which is what we're examining in this book. And Mehrabian's research is now fifty years old and dealt with a small number of subjects. It should not be the most cited statistic in public speaking.

Where does this leave us?

It is silly to assign percentages to the importance of our words, voice, and body language. In the end, they are all important.

How we speak can make a difference, so we should focus on it. Research suggests speakers are more persuasive when they speak at higher volumes and vary their volume.[4] One theory for why this works is that it projects confidence, and the listener thinks "they sound confident, so they must be right." Because we want to be persuasive, we should do this.

But this doesn't mean our voice is the most important thing, so we should not obsess endlessly about it. With delivery, the most important thing is to

2. Interview with Albert Mehrabian, MediaTrainingCompany YouTube Page (Nov. 23, 2021), https://www.youtube.com/watch?v=bPi7GmQIjB8.

3. Albert Mehrabian, *"Silent Messages"—A Wealth of Information About Nonverbal Communication (Body Language)*, http://www.kaaj.com/psych/smorder.html (last visited April 9, 2025).

4. Abigail B. Van Zant & Jonah Berger, *How the Voice Persuades*, 116 J. Personality & Soc. Psychol. 682 (2019).

talk in a pleasant voice that is easy to understand—good volume, enunciated words, an easy-to-follow pace, and good pitch variance (avoid monotone).

It's so simple it seems obvious, but people get these things wrong all the time. So this chapter teaches us how to improve our vocal delivery.

The title of this chapter is "bring *your* best voice." The word "your" is emphasized for a reason. It is emphasized because I do not want anyone to think they need a complete voice makeover to have good vocal delivery.

The goal isn't to develop a voice like Morgan Freeman or Meryl Streep. And we don't need to put in effort like Bradley Cooper, who spent six months lowering his voice by an octave for his role in *A Star Is Born*.

Rather, this chapter focuses on small, concrete things that can make the voice we were born with sound better, with a little practice and attention. Remember, the goal is to sound pleasant and easy to understand. We can start just trying to mumble less than we do when we talk casually with our close friends.

7.1 Keep Your Volume, Pace, and Pitch in the Sweet Spot

Let's get the obvious but obligatory advice out of the way.

When it comes to three parts of our voice—our volume, pace, and pitch—we're dealing with the "Goldilocks principle." We want to find a sweet spot in the middle where each one is just right.

Don't talk too loud or too quiet, too fast or too slow, or too high or too low.

Our **volume** should be in a range where everyone can hear us clearly without suffering ear damage. This means we should project as much as the room requires but not yell.

Our **speed** should be between 120 and 170 words per minute.

And our **pitch** should mostly be in the middle of our vocal range (with some variety). Don't let your dominant pitch be your high falsetto voice or the vocal fry at the bottom of your range.

If you're bad at any of these things, you will see it on your audience's faces, if you pay attention. If you're unsure, find people you trust—who are comfortable being honest and open with you—and ask them. (If you don't have those people in your life, that's a different problem outside the scope of this book.)

All three things are easy to get better at with practice. You can download apps that help you track your volume, speed, and pitch. The latest version of

Figure 8: PowerPoint's "Rehearse with Coach" Feature

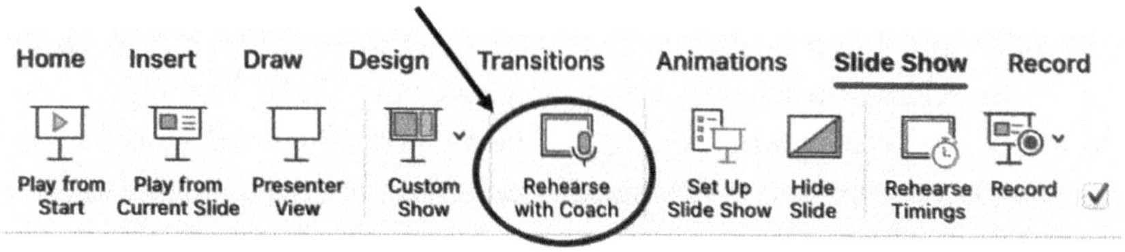

PowerPoint comes with a "Rehearse with Coach" option in the "Slide Show" menu that will give you feedback on these components (see Figure 8).

To illustrate the value of this tool, Figure 9 shows the type of "Rehearsal Report" PowerPoint provides, with notes on your pace, pitch, fillers, and originality.

Sometimes I talk to people who do not like the natural pitch of their voice; usually they complain it's too high. If this is you, I do not recommend forcing yourself to talk unnaturally lower or working to change your vocal range. It is very hard to do, and there are much easier ways to make yourself sound better at your natural pitch. Trust me; keep reading.

7.2 Use Variety, Pauses, and Tone to Reach the Next Level

The fastest way to improve our natural speaking voice is to focus on three things: vocal variety, better pauses, and an enthusiastic, conversational tone.

No matter what your natural pitch is, your voice will sound dramatically better if you master these three things. This is where you will see the biggest returns, so this is where you should focus. When you're done, you may wonder why you didn't like your voice to begin with.

Variety

Let's start with vocal variety—talking at different volumes, speeds, and pitches. This is what makes us interesting to listen to. And as we all know now, the first mission in public speaking is to not be boring.

As speakers, we communicate with sounds. So we should borrow from things that sound good to the ear, like music. Good music has variety—mel-

Figure 9: Example of PowerPoint "Rehearsal Report"

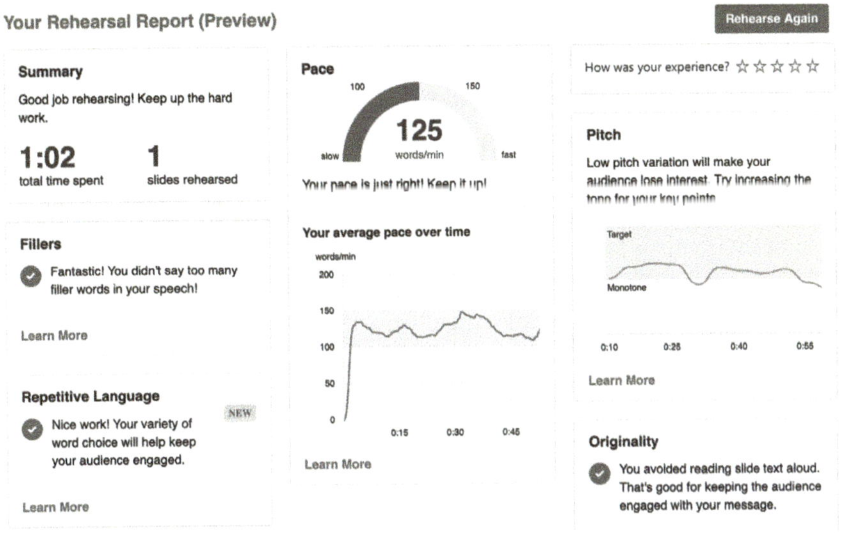

odies that move between notes at different pitches, tempos that speed up and slow down, quiet moments followed by louder ones (the rock band Nirvana wrote a dozen hits that followed the "loud-quiet-loud" format). Nothing stops us from bringing these same dynamics to our speaking voices.

Research suggests that vocal variety also boosts our credibility.[5] This makes intuitive sense. People who talk too fast all the time seem nervous. People who talk too slowly seem clueless and out-of-touch. So do people who talk too loudly or too softly—they seem unaware of everyone else in the room.

But speakers who vary these things in interesting ways—for example, softening their voice to make us lean closer for a big, emotional point—can grip us. It shows their command of their voice, their content, and the room. It shows that they are like a musician who knows how to play their instrument, and the audience relaxes and settles into their seat because they know they are in for something enjoyable to listen to.

Successful attention getters use these tools all the time. Let's talk about YouTubers for a second.

A guy named Jimmy Donaldson—"MrBeast" on YouTube—is the most successful one. He has more than 380 million subscribers to his YouTube

5. Alex Van Zant & Jonah Berger, *How the Voice Persuades*, 116 J. PERSONALITY & SOC. PSYCHOL. 682 (2019).

channel, which is greater than the entire population of the United States. He is an expert at holding attention.

Watch his videos and you will notice that he talks a little funny. He over-enunciates words. He elongates vowels. He changes pace often. And he uses lots of intonation (which means he varies his pitch). The pure, aesthetic quality of his voice isn't anything like Morgan Freeman's, yet he has built an enormous audience that can't get enough of him.

Other successful YouTubers talk this way too, especially ones who spend most of their videos talking straight to the camera.

This is such a phenomenon that linguists have a name for it—"YouTube voice."[6] Linguists say that people actually use these speech devices all the time to grab attention, especially when it's just them talking to a camera. Jon Stewart uses some on *The Daily Show*, to a lesser degree. Newscasters do too.

Naomi Baron, a professor of linguistics at American University, says changing pace is an especially effective way to keep people interested.[7] This checks out with some research. For example, consultant Vanessa Van Edwards studied famous TED Talks and found that the more vocal variety a speaker had, the more views they had.[8]

I'm not telling you to bring YouTube voice to your legal presentations. If you did, you'd get weird looks. But I am telling you to adopt a similar mindset about playing with your voice, and to pay attention to how successful attention-getters use their voice.

Your voice is a tool to keep the audience's attention, and the best way to use it is to vary it. Public speakers need to earn the audience's attention every minute, so why not take some lessons from other performers who need to do the same thing?

Record yourself using more vocal variety than you normally do—and really go for it. No one else is listening. This is a low-stakes time to play around. Then listen to the recording. This is the hard part for most people, but I promise you will like what you hear, at least more than past recordings.

Many people think it's the tone of their voice they don't like, but I believe it has more to do with the lack of variety in their voice. Most people talk

6. Julie Beck, *The Linguistics of "YouTube Voice,"* The Atlantic (Dec. 7, 2015), https://www.theatlantic.com/technology/archive/2015/12/the-linguistics-of-youtube-voice/418962/.

7. *Id.*

8. Vanessa Van Edwards, *6 Secrets of a Successful TED Talk* (Mar. 24, 2025), https://www.scienceofpeople.com/secrets-of-a-successful-ted-talk/.

mostly one way. That's why people are labeled "fast talkers" or "slow talkers." As "soft-spoken" or "authoritative." And when you talk just one way, you don't sound like the interesting people we like listening to on radio, tv, podcasts, or YouTube.

This problem isn't new. It was a problem in the late 1800s too. As the late trial lawyer Henry S. Wilcox said:

> Many speakers soon after starting reach a monotone pitched about three notes above the ordinary talking key and hold the pitch without variation until the end of their address. This has the most soporific effect upon the court and makes them wish for a bed where they might attain to a state of unconsciousness.[9]

To counteract this, trial advocacy trainers Brian Johnson and Marsha Hunter encourage people to obey the "Law of Opposites."[10] Simply, figure out what you do the most of, and do more of the opposite. If you often talk fast, talk slower when you want to emphasize an important point. If you talk loudly, talk softer for emphasis. And if you often talk at one pitch, find some other ones to hit (still near the middle of your natural range).

Johnson and Hunter tell us to "[s]urprise your jury and mix up your choices to keep your voice and presentation from becoming predictable, repetitive, and ultimately, boring."[11]

Improving our vocal variety starts with being present and aware of the sounds we are making. This leads us to our next technique—better pauses—because no technique helps us become more present during a speech than building in planned pauses.

Better Pauses

Because many people are nervous when they speak publicly, they forget to pause. Instead, their adrenaline fuels them to talk at a constant rate until it's over and they can get off the stage. This is a big problem, for four reasons.

First, pausing unlocks our vocal variety. Each time we pause, it gives us a chance to do something different—speed up, slow down, get louder, go softer.

---

9. Quoted in SCALIA & GARNER, cited above in Chapter 1, note 8, at 142.
10. JOHNSON & HUNTER, cited above in Chapter 5, note 5, at 164.
11. *Id.*

But if we never pause, it is very hard to switch gears. Instead, we'll be stuck in one and bore our audience, who craves variety.

Second, pausing makes it easier for our audience to process and understand what we're saying. Remember, in Chapter 4.2 we discussed how people need to actively think about new information—and build connections between the new information and what they already know—to learn. Building in more pauses—even if just a half-second long—helps them do that.

Third, pausing has a powerful effect on how our audience perceives us. They think we're more credible. Wharton professor Jonah Berger did a study where half the participants listened to a speaker talking without pauses, and the other half listened to the same speaker talk with pauses.[12] The second group liked the speaker more.

Berger believes the reason is that "when someone pauses while speaking, we have a tendency to assent—basically to agree with them."[13] In those moments, we aren't literally saying, "I agree with you," but we might be nodding our head to tell the speaker that we've got it, "keep going." But later, when we reflect on the experience, we believe that we spent a lot of time agreeing with the speaker and thus think more positively about them. According to Berger, "pausing increases our impact."

Fourth, pausing is one of the best ways to regain and hold attention because it creates tension and suspense. It is a great irony that our best tool to get people to focus on us is to stop talking. Try it and see. If you stop talking for long enough during a closing argument, any juror who is looking down or away from you will come right back. They'll notice the pause in their subconscious and turn their attention back to you to see what happened—why aren't you talking anymore? Did they miss something important? It is cliché, but silence is deafening.

Professor Berger says President Barack Obama did a "great job of using pauses to draw attention."[14] Ronald Reagan—a professional actor, also dubbed the "Great Communicator"—was a great pauser too.

As with all parts of our voice, we want to find the right balance and not pause too much or for too long because that can hurt our credibility. But most

12. Alex Van Zant, Jonah A. Berger, Grant M. Packard & Harry Wang, *The Power of Pausing in Conversation* (Jan. 31, 2025) (unpublished manuscript), https://ssrn.com/abstract=5119651.

13. Interview with Jonah Berger, in *This Advice Will Make You More Persuasive*, Nudge Podcast (Jan. 8, 2024).

14. *Id.*

of us don't have this problem. Research suggests four seconds or more is when pausing feels too long.[15] Most of us never pause that long, unless we've completely forgotten what to say. Most of us pause for less than one second. Great speakers pause for two or three.[16]

We also don't pause enough. TED speaker Noah Zandan analyzed over 4,000 spoken communication samples and the data showed "that the average speaker only uses 3.5 pauses per minute, and that's not enough."[17]

By contrast, in President Obama's 2017 farewell speech, he often used more than 10 pauses per minute, most for one second or longer.[18] Many of his other speeches are the same.

So how do we pause more?

The advice we got in Chapter 5.1 about speaking in phrases, not whole sentences, is a good start. Speaking in phrases builds in more opportunities to pause at natural points—for example, where someone reading the same language would expect to see a comma or other punctuation mark.

We should also practice our pauses when rehearsing, and we should write reminders to ourselves to pause. For many people, this is a better reminder than one to "slow down." University of Michigan law professor Patrick Barry encourages his students to write "PAUSE" on their notes—not just once, but "between every paragraph, as well as between many of your key sentences and phrases."[19] He, too, is a fan of using well-planned pauses to boost your poise and charisma. He writes that an effective speaker isn't someone who has people hanging on their every word, but one who has them hanging on their "every pause."[20]

In short, pause more. It puts you in the moment and unlocks the full potential of your vocal delivery.

15. Kristina Lundholm Fors, *Pauses Can Make or Break a Conversation*, U. Gothenberg (Sept. 7, 2015), https://www.gu.se/en/news/pauses-can-make-or-break-a-conversation.

16. Noah Dandan, *How to Stop Saying "Um," "Ah," and "You Know,"* Harv. Bus. Rev. (Aug. 1, 2018), https://hbr.org/2018/08/how-to-stop-saying-um-ah-and-you-know.

17. *Id.*

18. Interview with Jonah Berger, cited above in note 13.

19. Patrick Barry, cited above in Chapter 4, note 26, at 10.

20. *Id.* at 11.

Tone

Research shows our audience likes two things when it comes to our tone of voice—when we're enthusiastic[21] and when we're conversational.[22] Both qualities make us better understood and appear more favorable to the audience.

I probably didn't need to cite research to tell you this. Just think about what you would want from a speaker. Would you want them to be dull and uninterested? Would you want them to be stiff and overly formal? I'm still waiting for someone to answer "yes" to these questions.

Yet we don't always bring the desired qualities to our presentations.

Sometimes our nerves—or dread of talking to an audience—zap our enthusiasm for our subject. Maybe we were excited when we first agreed to present or take a trial, but when the moment gets closer our nerves kick in. We regret not preparing more. And we don't like the physiological effect on our bodies. So suddenly we don't want to be there. This shows up in our tone of voice.

This can be hard to overcome, but it helps to remember that it's not about us, it's about them. In his excellent public speaking book, *I Have Something to Say*, speech consultant John Bowe describes shyness as "little more than selfishness."[23] His book encourages speakers to stop thinking so much about themselves and how others see them and instead consider the audience and how they hear.[24]

This is harsh advice. But if we put the audience's needs above ours—and remember that they like enthusiasm—it can get us in a better state of mind. This doesn't mean we should embody false enthusiasm. Instead, we should find the enthusiasm we once had—because it is what our audience wants.

Ralph Waldo Emerson said, "Nothing great was ever achieved without enthusiasm." This quote captures a core truth. Becoming a lawyer requires hard work and dedication. I would guess you had enthusiasm for it at some stage. It can also be noble work and extremely important to our clients. So we have many reasons to be enthusiastic about what we do. We should find them and reflect them in our speaking voices. If we aren't excited to be there, why should the audience be?

---

21. Su-Mae Tan, Si Kew, Tze Wei Liew & Teck Ming Tan, *Does Speaker's Voice Enthusiasm Affect Social Cue, Cognitive Load and Transfer in Multimedia Learning?*, 121 INFO. & LEARNING SCI. 117 (2020).

22. MAYER, cited above in Chapter 3, note 1, at 322.

23. JOHN BOWE, I HAVE SOMETHING TO SAY 101 (2020).

24. *Id.* at 85.

The other mistake we make with tone is being too formal. This usually comes from thinking we need to act like a lawyer. We don't.

Maybe it comes from imposter syndrome or fearing people won't think we're smart if we talk the way we normally do. Fortunately, the research says we can relax about this.

It may seem counterintuitive but when we use more complicated language, we come across as less intelligent.[25] Being overly formal also puts extra distance between us and the audience, and it makes us less relatable. We can be closer to our normal, conversational self than we think.

In the end, just show up ready to have an enthusiastic conversation with your friends. It sounds simple, but many people mess it up.

7.3 Avoid These Things That Kill Your Clarity and Credibility

It's time to talk about clarity and credibility. Here are the things that kill it:

- Mumbling and poor enunciation
- Filler words (ums, uhs, likes, ahs, you knows, justs, you sees, basically, literally)
- Verbal ticks (throat clearing, sniffing, repeated speech)
- Powerless language (lots of hedging, saying "I think," "I guess," "sort of," "kinda," "it seems," "in my opinion")
- Upspeak (raising our pitch at the end of sentences)

These aren't just stylistically bad. Research shows that they make us less persuasive, less credible, and harder to understand.[26] One reason is that they are all distracting. None of them furthers our message. They are "extraneous information" our audience needs to process and thus they make our message less potent. If we eliminate them, the audience can instead spend their brain energy on our core message. That's what we want.

How do we avoid them?

25. Brown et al., cited above in Chapter 4, note 4.

26. D.R. Seals & M.E. Coppock, *We, Um, Have, Like, a Problem: Excessive Use of Fillers in Scientific Speech*, 46 Adv. Physiol. Educ. 615 (2022); William M. O'Barr, Linguistic Evidence: Language, Power, and Strategy in the Courtroom (1982).

If you have a mumbling problem, you need to warm up your articulators before you present. Your articulators are the parts of your mouth, nose, and throat that produce speech. Like all muscles in the body, they perform better after a few warm-up exercises, which draw blood to the area, ease tension, and make everything fire more precisely.

The best speech warm-ups are tongue twisters. Things like: "she sells seashells by the seashore."

Or:

Peter Piper picked a peck of pickled peppers.
A peck of pickled peppers Peter Piper picked.
If Peter Piper picked a peck of pickled peppers,
where's the peck of pickled peppers Peter Piper picked?

If you're bored with these, use this fresh one by comedian Elle Cordova about a duck named Quincy who is talented at heckling:

> Quincy the quirky quacker was a quantum cracking hacker. He quaintly quacked in qubits while he cached a queue of crackers. Critics quickly quibbled over Quincy's quantum drivel. Was he a quack, a quantum hack or a crafty quacking hacker?[27]

Or use this one I made about a lawyer named Larry:

> Lofty lawyer Larry litigates lawsuits loosely. Larry leaves legal loopholes lurking largely, while wily witness Wendy weaves words wondrously. But we must wonder about wacky witness William, who's willfully wavering words warrant widespread worry.

In our digital age—with more work from home and disconnection—people have a mumbling problem. Many of us spend less time around strangers than we used to. Thus we mumble through the day with loved ones and close friends. We need to break this habit before we go on stage by warming up our voice.

To stop saying filler words and powerless hedges we need to be more present when we speak and embrace the silence created by our pauses. We usually insert filler to fill the silence when we're thinking of what to say next. If we replace the fillers with pauses, we sound more confident and in control rather than distracting our audience.

27. Elle Cordova, *Tongue Twisters*, YouTube (Jan. 5, 2025), https://www.youtube.com/watch?v=iPHFNj9sP4E.

To get in the habit, I recommend building a planned pause into your speech as early as possible, such as: "Hi." **PAUSE.**

And practice, practice, practice. Many apps and software programs—including PowerPoint—have features that will track and score these things. At every Toastmasters meeting (one of the world's largest public speaking organizations), someone called an "Ah-Counter" tracks everyone's use of filler words. Luckily, technology now gives us an Ah-Counter in our pocket every time we talk.

Implementing all the advice in this book can be a lot to start. But as you improve each piece, the game will slow down for you. Adopt a growth mindset and remember most people have not had this training.

You don't need to be Morgan Freeman or Meryl Streep. You just need to talk in a pleasant way that is easy to understand. With a little work and attention, anyone can get there.

Quick Tip from an Advocate

Howard King is the managing partner of King, Holmes, Paterno & Soriano, LLP in Los Angeles. The Hollywood Reporter named him one of the "Power 100 Lawyers in Entertainment," and he has handled many historic cases, including serving as lead counsel in *Metallica v. Napster*. I asked him for a tip about connecting with the jury. Here is what he said:

> Slow down and tell your story with understated passion, humility, and some humor. Make an inside joke that recalls something that happened during trial—maybe a mistake you made that got a laugh or showed your vulnerability.
>
> Also, don't talk like a stereotypical lawyer. A juror once wrote me a note after a trial that said he appreciated how I spoke more like a rabbi than a lawyer and explained how their verdict would affect real people.
>
> Finally, don't write out your closing argument word for word. Just write out bullet points and talk to those points, even if you think that won't be as smooth as reading a full script you prepared. Being a little rough gets you more attention from most juries, who can get lulled into boredom by a smooth, but canned, speech.

8

Rule Eight: No Weird Body Language

Last chapter, we learned there is no hard support for the claim that our nonverbal communication—our voice and body language—is 93 percent more important than the words we use. Body language is not a dark art that we can use to hypnotize our audiences and take over their minds, content be damned. Still, body language is important in communication, and we should use it to support our message the best we can.

This chapter's advice goes together with last chapter's advice about how to use our voice. This is because research says that our voices and body gestures are linked.[1] They move together—our gesturing speeds up and slows down in tandem with our voices.

Body language expert Dr. Carol Kinsey Goman says, "Gesture is really linked to speech, and gesturing while you talk can really power up your thinking. Gesturing can help people form clearer thoughts, speak in tighter sentences, and use more declarative language."[2]

---

1. Wim Pouw & Susanne Fuchs, *Origins of Vocal-Entangled Gesture*, 141 Neurosci. & Biobehav. Rev. 104836 (2022).

2. Carolyn Gregoire, *The Fascinating Science Behind 'Talking' With Your Hands*, Huffington Post (Feb. 4, 2016), https://www.huffpost.com/entry/talking-with-hands-gestures_n_56afcfaae4b0b8d7c230414e.

If our voice lacks variety, more gesturing can help. If we sound robotic and unnatural, we should look at whether we are gesturing naturally or awkwardly suppressing our gestures.

Research also shows that gestures help our audience process and understand our communication—sometimes twice as well.[3] And it says having good posture might help us look and feel more confident (standing tall with shoulders back and feet firmly planted).[4]

So we need to pay attention to our body language and make sure it is working for us, not against us. This chapter gives some tips.

8.1 Know What to Do with Your Hands

In a classic scene from the 2006 comedy *Talladega Nights*, Will Ferrell's character Ricky Bobby gives his first on-camera interview, and it is derailed because Ricky doesn't know what to do with his hands. He grabs the microphone awkwardly, puts his hands too close to his face and muffles his voice, and keeps bringing his hands into the shot even after the interviewer moves them away. "I'm not sure what to do with my hands," he says.

People love this scene because it captures something many can relate to. When the spotlight is on us, we become hyper aware of our hands and don't know what to do with them.

So what should we do with our hands?

I have reviewed dozens of public speaking guides, videos, and studies on this. It comes down to three things.

First, we should gesture, *a lot*. The gestures should be synched with our vocal message. When we're talking, we should be gesturing; when we're not, our hands should be at rest. When we're referring to ourselves, we should touch our chest. When we're referring to the audience, we should extend our palms toward them.

When we're referring to a number between 1 and 5, we should hold up the same number of fingers. When we want to emphasize a point, we should chop our hands. When we're referring to something large, we should show it by

3. Adam Kendon, ed., *Gesture and Understanding in Social Interaction*, 27 Res. on Lang. & Soc. Interaction 3 (1994) (special edition).

4. D.R. Carney, A.J. Cuddy & A.J. Yap, *Power Posing: Brief Nonverbal Displays Affect Neuroendocrine Levels and Risk Tolerance*, 21 Psychol. Sci. 1363 (2010).

holding our hands wide apart. When we're referring to something small, we should show it by pinching our fingers close together.

When we're talking about something physical a witness did—like throwing a punch or signing a contract—we should pantomime their conduct. When we're talking about two competing ideas, we should put them on opposite ends of an imaginary shelf in front of us.

Many of us do these things in normal conversation. If that's you, great. Mimic your normal gesturing pattern.

Sometimes when we are on stage, we forget to do this and suppress our gestures. A good way to break this habit is to build in one planned gesture at the very beginning of the talk. This can be enough to get your natural flow going. Once you do this, you will also find yourself talking with better vocal variety. Again, our voice and body are connected. As top communication coach Vinh Giang says, "A monotone voice comes from a monotone body." Let your hands move freely and don't suppress them by clinging to the lectern or clutching an object.

If you struggle with gesturing naturally, watch videos of news and weathercasters. Pay attention to the way they gesture. They are the best in the business. Note what they do and copy it. Al Roker from NBC's *Today Show* is one of the best to watch and you can find many videos of him online. (Do not mimic modern late-night show hosts like Stephen Colbert and Jimmy Kimmel—they put their hand in their pockets a lot, which most experts don't recommend.)

You will see that news and weathercasters all gesture frequently. They do this because it works. Communication expert Vanessa Van Edwards analyzed hundreds of hours of TED Talks looking for patterns in the most and least popular talks. She found that the most popular talks were also the ones where the speakers used their hands the most.[5] In 18 minutes, these speakers used almost twice as many hand gestures as the speakers with the least popular talks.

Van Edwards says hand gestures work because they build trust. She—and others—claim this goes back to our early ancestors. When we show our hands, it signals we're not holding any weapons. This is why open-palm gestures are particularly recommended.

---

5. Jena McGregor & Shelly Tan, *What to do With Your Hands When Speaking in Public*, Washington Post (Nov. 17, 2015), https://www.washingtonpost.com/news/on-leadership/wp/2015/11/17/what-to-do-with-your-hands-when-speaking-in-public/; Van Edwards, cited above in Chapter 7, note 8.

Figure 10: The Gesture Zone

Hand gestures also make us easier to understand. Van Edwards says this is because we are giving "two explanations in one, and the brain loves that."[6] It also shows the audience that we know our content well. Every movement is intentional and matches the message.

In short, we should support our words with our gestures and do it often.

Second, we should keep the range of our gestures between our belly button and our shoulders and not go too wide. Think of it as a rectangle that is two feet tall and four feet wide, like we see in Figure 10.

This avoids drawing our audience's attention to anything below our belt, and it keeps our hands from blocking our face. Every public speaking expert agrees on this, but they call it different names—the "strike zone,"[7] the "power

6. McGregor & Tan, cited above in note 5.
7. *Id.*

Figure 11: The Gesture Zone (seated and on camera)

sphere,"[8] and the "zone of gesture"[9] are three. (I guess I need my own. How about the "strength sector?" Never mind.)

This is a natural zone to gesture in. Using the entire space also ensures our gestures are big enough to be easily seen without looking over the top or comical. Again, watch news and weathercasters. They all gesture in this zone.

When we talk virtually—which is more common these days—we also need to make sure our gestures can be seen on camera. If we are seated talking to the computer, we likely need to shrink the zone because gestures closer to our waist will fall outside the camera view. So for these situations, the vertical line of the rectangle should go from your mid-chest to shoulders (see Figure 11). Many people forget to gesture (or gesture invisibly) online, which detracts from their performance.

8. Vinh Giang, *Simple Rule for Using Hand Gestures!* (Sept. 9, 2024), https://www.youtube.com/watch?v=TTCxDsByxZk.

9. Johnson & Hunter, cited above in Chapter 5, note 5, at 30.

Third, we need to keep our hands in the right place when we're not using them. In other words, a good resting position. The best place is right in front of our belly button, loosely touching or close together. This means we should bend our arms at the elbow, creating a ninety-degree angle, and keep our hands a few inches in front of us. If you're not sure what this looks like, watch Al Roker again. See where he rests his hands? That's the place.

Figure 12 shows another example.

Experts agree on this too.[10] Media trainer Bill McGowan says it works because it looks natural and lets you gesture easier. "There's never a long distance for [your hands] to travel, so your gestures don't become distracting."[11]

Brian Johnson calls this the "invisible ready position."[12] It looks so natural that most observers don't notice it.

Just as important is avoiding awkward resting positions—the "fig leaf" (in front of the groin), behind the back, arms crossed, in our pockets, on our hips, or at our sides. Each of these positions makes it harder to gesture. They also make us look nervous, awkward, uncomfortable, or like we have something to hide.

Use the news/weathercaster ready position. They figured this out a long time ago, so we don't have to.

In short, what we should do with our hands comes down to three things—(1) gesturing a lot, (2) gesturing in the gesture zone, and (3) keeping our hands in the invisible ready position when we're not gesturing. It's as simple as 1-2-3.

EXAMPLE: JOHNNIE COCHRAN

Johnnie Cochran has been called a "master of gesture" because he frequently used his hands to complement his vocal message.[13]

In his opening statement in the O.J. Simpson trial, when he questioned the prosecution's case, Cochran touched his fingers to his chin with a thoughtful look, signaling to the jury that they, too, should think hard about what he was saying. He moved his hands in rhythm with his words to keep

---

10. McGowan, cited above in Chapter 1, note 6, at 117; Johnson & Hunter, cited above in Chapter 5, note 5, at 34.

11. McGowan, cited above in Chapter 1, note 6, at 117.

12. Johnson & Hunter, cited above in Chapter 5, note 5, at 35.

13. *The Defense Opening*, in Trial Communication Skills § 36:4 (2d ed.)

Figure 12: The Ready Position

the jury engaged. And he did all this even though he was standing behind a lectern. He did not let it "be a barrier between him and the jury. When he wanted to get things across to the jury, he leaned all the way across the podium, so that he was physically close to the jurors."[14]

This helped him create a strong connection with the jurors. He was not delivering a canned speech from the lectern to a distant audience. He was talking directly to them.

14. *Id.*

8.2 Make Eye Contact and Smile

Make eye contact with your audience and smile.

Ask any person what makes someone else likable, and they will come up with these two things. Research also confirms them. More eye contact and more smiles make us more likable and thus more persuasive.[15]

If it's so simple, why do we get it wrong?

Because we are too wedded to our notes.

If we go to trial infrequently, we aren't used to talking on our feet and we are afraid we might forget our points, so we put them on paper and read them. We are also wordsmiths, obsessed with saying everything perfectly. We fall in love with the perfect word formulations we come up with late at night and want to repeat them verbatim in court. So we read a script.

The problem is this destroys our chance to connect with the jury or audience, which is the whole reason for speaking.

Remember, the presentation is about *them*, not us. Reading a script and not making eye contact sends the wrong message. It tells them we are more interested in showing off all the smart points we thought of than speaking directly to them and their needs. We are more interested in connecting with our notes than the audience.

People also associate bad eye contact with deception. Those who don't look us in the eyes have something to hide. We can test this with any kid we suspect of lying. When they aren't telling the truth, they look away.

This means we need to ditch our notes. If this thought produces anxiety, I promise the connection gained with the audience will more than make up for forgetting a few perfect words. The audience will like us more and be more willing to consider our points. They will feel we care about them and be more invested in our talk. And they will want us to succeed.

Connecting with the audience also helps us see when things aren't landing, and when we might need to adjust. If we see pained or confused faces, we might realize that we are talking too fast or using unfamiliar words and fix it. If we are looking down at a script, we will miss these cues and be unable to fix anything in the moment.

Enron prosecutor John Hueston understands how critical this is. He tells new attorneys to never read their opening statements.[16] When he trained trial

---

15. Judee K. Burgoon et al., *Nonverbal Behaviors, Persuasion & Credibility*, 17 Hum. Comm. Res. 140, 151–153 (1990).

16. Hueston, cited above in Chapter 2, note 22.

lawyers at the United States Attorney's Office, he promised that if he caught them reading an opening statement in court, he would walk up and pull away the notes. Apparently, it happened once. The attorney stumbled for a moment but improved.

According to Hueston:

> The decision to read your opening is a decision to forego a personal connection with your jury. And your written work has a metric and cadence distinct from natural verbal communication. Better to forget some words, appear human and make a genuine connection than to read a rehearsed statement.[17]

Bryan Garner and the late Supreme Court Justice Antonin Scalia give similar advice for talking to judges: "When you're standing in court, look at the judge. In the eye. That's the only way to establish the relationship you want. You are advising the judge, not merely speaking in the same room."[18]

They also say to never read your argument. In the Supreme Court, the Chief Justice has been known to interrupt counsel who read.[19] And remember, at an oral argument, the lectern doesn't have a vote. The judges do. So look at them.

The other reason we make bad eye contact, especially with jurors, is that they give us stoic facial expressions back. Part of this may be due to the formal courtroom environment and the judge's instructions that jurors are not to have any communication with the attorneys. Whatever the reason, jurors don't always give us the positive facial feedback we crave, and this makes us uncomfortable.

My advice is, don't worry about it. This is normal in trials. It shouldn't stop us from making eye contact. And the good news is we have more than one juror to look at—usually between six and twelve. We want to spread our eye contact around, so we only need to hold it with each person for a few seconds. One study suggests two to five seconds is the ideal length.[20] Anything less than one second is too shifty and anything more than nine is too creepy. Making good eye contact—even when staring down a bunch of poker faces—is the ultimate sign of confidence.

---

17. *Id.*

18. SCALIA & GARNER, cited above in Chapter 1, note 8, at 178.

19. *Id.* at 181.

20. N. Binetti et al., *Pupil Response Hazard Rates Predict Perceived Gaze Durations*, 7 SCI. REP. 3969 (2017).

We also need to smile because it makes us more engaging, likable, and persuasive. Research suggests people who smile more are thought to be more intelligent.[21] It also says emotions and facial expressions are contagious.[22] So if we want our audience to respond enthusiastically to our message, we need to deliver it enthusiastically.

Great teachers understand this. In the seminal teaching guide, *How Learning Works*, former Carnegie Melon professor Susan Ambrose and her colleagues advise:

> Even if students are not initially attracted to or interested in your [subject], don't be afraid to let your excitement ... show. Your enthusiasm might raise students' curiosity and motivate them to find out what excites you about the subject, leading them to engage more deeply than they had initially planned or discover the value they had overlooked.[23]

Similarly, Michigan law professor Patrick Barry tells his public speaking students to "smile more than you think appropriate."[24]

This has two important caveats.

First, we want real, genuine-looking smiles—not forced fake ones or big goofy ones. Sincere smiles raise our cheeks and engage the muscles around our eyes, causing wrinkles on the outside—that is, "crow's feet."[25] These are the smiles that work—meaning they make us appear more likeable, trustworthy, and competent.[26] Some people call them "Duchenne smiles" after a 19th-century French anatomist who noticed the cheek-muscle thing. I don't use that term, but now you know it. We can just call them natural smiles.

Ideally, we can channel our excitement and joy for our subject to produce a natural smile. But even if that's hard, research says we can deliberately produce natural-looking smiles.[27] We just need to practice smiling with our eyes. If we don't engage the eyes, the audience will tell we are faking it. And that's not good.

---

21. Van Edwards, cited above in Chapter 7, note 8.

22. L.-O. Lundqvist & U. Dimberg, *Facial Expressions Are Contagious*, 9 J. Psychophysiology 203 (1995).

23. Ambrose et al., cited above in Chapter 2, note 1, at 85.

24. Patrick Barry, cited above in Chapter 4, note 26, at 42.

25. Paul Ekman, *Fake Smile or Genuine Smile?*, Paul Ekman Group Blog, https://www.paulekman.com/blog/fake-smile-or-genuine-smile/.

26. Sarah Gunnery, Judith Hall & Mollie Ruben, *The Deliberate Duchenne Smile: Individual Differences in Expressive Control*, 37 J. Nonverbal Behav. 29 (2012).

27. *Id.*

To avoid overdoing it, courtroom delivery coach Cecilia Childress says, "Master a smile that is almost entirely composed of lips pressed together with much eye crinkling, as if your dignity compels you to hold back a smile."[28] This can be enough to let jurors, judges, and clients see that you like them.

Second, our facial impressions need to match our message, and some messages make it inappropriate to smile. If we are talking about something tragic, deeply upsetting, or anger-inducing—think a wrongful death case—we should obviously not be smiling.

Thus, how often we smile should depend on the nature of our case or subject. Still, even the most serious subjects provide *some* opportunities to smile. When they appear, take advantage of them. This shows our audience we like them, and it can make us appear more competent and persuasive.

Quick Tip from a Retired Judge

The Honorable Patrick J. Walsh (Ret.) served as the Chief Magistrate Judge on the U.S. District Court for the Central District of California and is now a private mediator and arbitrator. I asked him for a tip on how to connect with the jury in the opening statement and closing argument. This is what he said:

> The goal of opening and closing is to communicate with the jurors on an interpersonal level, just as you would with any person or group you wanted to persuade. This requires that you make eye contact with the jurors and avoid reading from your notes. Particularly in opening, jurors are not going to pick up on a lot of the details you're sharing with them. What they will pick up on is that you know the case inside and out and that you are confident in your position. This will be communicated by your words and actions in opening and will help you later in the trial.

28. Celia W. Childress, *Body Language for Trial Lawyers: Persuasive Gestures, Postures, and Foot Movement in the Courtroom*, 84 Am. Jur. Trials 1 (2008).

8.3 Find and Eliminate Unconscious Things That Make You Look Nervous

When we are new to public speaking—or don't exercise the skills regularly—we do unconscious things with our bodies that make us look nervous. We look around too much, fidget with our hands, play with objects, sway back and forth, lean to one side, touch our face, tap things, and so on.

This is a problem because credibility is a perception of confidence. It isn't something that lives permanently inside us. It exists in the minds of our audience based on the perception we give off. If we exhibit nervous behaviors, we won't be seen as credible, no matter how much expert knowledge we have in our subject.

Shakespeare's play *Othello* teaches us a good lesson about this. In the climax of the play, Othello suspects his wife, Desdemona, has been unfaithful to him and he questions her. She denies it but is crying and anxious. Othello interprets her emotions as evidence she is lying, so he murders her. He learns shortly after that she was telling the truth.

Othello misinterpreted Desdemona's anguish as a sign of guilt, when it was instead caused by her fear Othello would not believe her. Psychologists call this "Othello error"—when someone tells the truth, but their nonverbal behavior causes them to be disbelieved.

This teaches us that there are two ways to speak the truth—with confidence and without it.

When we speak without confidence, it appears in our body language, facial expressions, and tone of voice. Because these behaviors are often unconscious, the best way to discover them is to record ourselves and watch the tape. Once we know they exist, we can fix them.

Communication coach Vinh Giang says that if he wanted to improve his communication skills, the first thing he would do is record himself every single day.[29] He says, "When you watch yourself back it's going to feel cringy but it's the fastest way you can spot what you need to improve."

We need to work through the discomfort and awkwardness to change. While changing behaviors can be hard, it is not impossible. K. Anders Ericsson, a leading psychologist on expert performance, says, "In pretty much any

---

29. Vinh Giang, *TOP 5 Things to Improve Your Communications Skills*, YouTube (Feb. 12, 2025), https://www.youtube.com/watch?v=-8xrWyS3CJw.

area of human endeavor, people have a tremendous capacity to improve their performance, as long as they train in the right way."[30]

His research also suggests that most expert performers are not born with natural talents the rest of us lack. The difference between them and us comes down to how much time they have deliberately tried to improve their skills.[31]

Most great public speakers were not born that way. They got there by working at it.

Some experts believe the easiest way to change a bad behavior is to replace it with a new one. So if you struggle with any of the nervous behaviors listed at the start of this section, make a conscious effort to replace them with purposeful hand gestures and the invisible resting position we discussed. Once you've modified your behavior enough times, the new behavior will become automatic. But it will only happen if you work at it.

Quick Tip from a Judge

The Honorable Damaris Diaz is a Los Angeles County Superior Court judge and former federal prosecutor. I asked her for a tip about establishing your credibility (ethos) in court. This is what she said:

> You are always "on." You are communicating every moment you are in the courthouse, whether you are giving a closing argument to the jury, conducting direct examination, sitting silently during court instructions, or even walking the hallway during a recess. Impressions are being made. Conduct yourself accordingly.

30. K. Anders Ericsson & Robert Pool, *Malcolm Gladwell Got Us Wrong: Our Research Was Key to the 10,000-Hour Rule, but Here's What Got Oversimplified*, Salon (Apr. 10, 2016), https://www.salon.com/2016/04/10/malcolm_gladwell_got_us_wrong_our_research_was_key_to_the_10000_hour_rule_but_heres_what_got_oversimplified/.

31. K. Anders Ericsson, Ralf T. Krampe & Clemens Tesch-Römer, *The Role of Deliberate Practice in the Acquisition of Expert Performance*, 100 Psychol. Rev. 363 (1993).

9

Rule Nine: Be a Real Human Being

As lawyers, our communication goal is rarely to just convey information to our audience. It is to impact them in some way—usually a significant one. We want jurors and judges to decide hotly contested disputes in our clients' favor. We want our colleagues to see us as experts in our niche and risk their reputations referring business to us. We want our clients to hire us to solve their biggest and most time-consuming problems.

It is hard to have this kind of influence on someone without first connecting with them. People make decisions for people they like and trust. People aren't computers. They're human beings. They like to be talked to by other human beings they can relate to.

Almost all the advice in this book so far will help us be relatable and connect with our audiences, but there's more to it. We need to talk like real people, which means being conversational and not overly formal. And we need to show humility and vulnerability, sometimes.

This chapter is about these things.

9.1 Talk Like a Normal Person

I've seen it many times. Because we went to law school, we think we can no longer talk like a normal person. Instead, we need to speak the new language we learned—legalese.

Nothing happens on an exact date anymore. It happens "on or about" some date.

Things don't happen "before" and "after" each other. They "occur" "prior" and "subsequent" to.

"Good" becomes "positive"; "bad" becomes "negative."

People no longer "hear" or "see" things. They "observe" and "perceive" them.

We no longer "start" anything. We "initiate" it.

"Cars" become "vehicles." And we don't "get out" of them. We "exit" them.

People "utilize" objects instead of "using" them.

We no longer tell people our points. We "submit" our points to them, just as "I am submitting all of this to you."

Sometimes we do this in the conditional mood, saying "I *would* submit to you," to make our point a little less certain and a little more abstract.

Other times, we "maintain" or "contend" our positions, instead of just saying them. (Side note: we also shouldn't "submit," "maintain," or "contend" things because it implies what we're saying isn't necessarily true.)

Our "main point" becomes the "gravamen" of our argument, which is also the law student's favorite code word to show they're smart. (I know because I used to be one of them.)

We no longer "need" to do something. It becomes "incumbent upon us" to do it.

A lot of this comes from law school professors assigning cases in stilted language from 100+ years ago. It also comes from feeling like we need to use special vocabulary to tell everyone that we are a lawyer.

As the late trial advocacy professor James McElhaney wrote:

> One of the reasons lawyers try so hard to sound like lawyers is that we suppose it gives us the trappings of credibility. If we know the magic words, we must know what we are talking about.[1]

Guess what?

---

1. James W. McElhaney, Litigation 373 (1995).

Our audience already knows we're lawyers. That's how the judge introduced us to the jury. That's why we get to sit at counsel table and make arguments from the lectern. That's why people came to our CLE. That's why our client wants to meet with us.

Also, none of this makes us seem smart. It's counterintuitive, but simple is smart. Using words only lawyers know—when there are good plain language alternatives—looks like we're overcompensating.

Studies have shown this. When people use complicated language, they come across as less smart.[2]

Judges think this too. In 1987, researchers asked judges to rate the quality and credibility of paragraphs written in legalese and plain English.[3] They rated the plain English ones higher.

Bryan Garner and Justice Scalia echo this advice in *Making Your Case: The Art of Persuading Judges*. Even when arguing at the Supreme Court, they recommend talking simply: "Avoid pretentious expression.... Your job is to make a complex case simple, not to make a simple case sound complex."[4]

Talking like a real person also holds the audience's attention better and improves their learning. Wharton professor Jonah Berger analyzed tens of thousands of pieces of content looking for clues about what held attention the best. One thing he found was that content that used familiar words did much better.[5] He even recommends using "car" instead of "automobile." Most people know both words, but "car" is "a more familiar word, and that familiarity makes it easier to process."[6]

In other research, educational psychologist Richard Mayer found people learn better when given information in a conversational rather than formal style.[7] He says "[w]hen learners feel that the [teacher] is talking to them, they are more likely to see the [teacher] as a conversational partner and therefore try harder to make sense of what the [teacher] is saying."

Finally, speaking like our audience is more persuasive. Advertisers know this well, and we should steal their insights because they are in the business of persuading people every day.

---

2. Brown et al., cited above in Chapter 4, note 4.

3. Robert W. Benson & Joan B. Kessler, *Legalese v. Plain English: An Empirical Study of Persuasion and Credibility in Appellate Brief Writing*, 20 Loy. L.A. L. Rev. 301 (1987).

4. Scalia & Garner, cited above in Chapter 1, note 8, at 182.

5. Berger et al., cited above in Chapter 1, note 19.

6. *Catching Eyes in the Attention Economy*, cited above in Chapter 1, note 19.

7. Mayer, cited above in Chapter 3, note 1, at 305.

David Ogilvy—the "Father of Advertising"—famously said: "If you're trying to persuade people to do something, or buy something, it seems to me you should use their language, the language they use every day, the language in which they think." Thus, the most successful ad campaigns use plain, simple words, like "Just Do It," "I'm Lovin' It," and "Melts in your mouth, not in your hand."

Imagine if these same slogans were written by lawyers using big words to show off: "Simply Perform the Task in Front of You," "I am Experiencing Strong Affection and Fondness for These Provisions," and "Dissolves in your oral cavity, not in your extremity." They'd be awful.

No one wants us to talk like a lawyer. It creates distance between us and the audience that stands in the way of connection. Our audience wants a friendly conversation, not a pompous oration.

Let's end with two examples—the first bad, and the second good.

EXAMPLE 1: *DEPP V. HEARD*

This is an example of legalese in a closing argument. Here is how Heard's attorney thanked the jury during his closing:

> Just as Ms. Vasquez and Mr. Chew did, I would like to extend my thanks to you on behalf of Amber and our whole legal team for the care and diligence with which you have served as jurors in this matter.

Translation = "Thank you for your hard work and service."

Heard's attorney used 41 words to say something he could have said in 8. He thanked the jury like a lawyer, not a real person.

This shows we need to unlearn our law school habits for something even as simple as saying thank you.

If you don't see all the awkward things in the statement, let me show you:

- **"Just as Ms. Vasquez and Mr. Chew did"**—There is no reason to point out that Depp's lawyers also said thank you. It makes it seem like he needs some justification to do it himself. He doesn't.
- **"I would like to extend my thanks"**—"Thank" is a verb used to express gratitude. Thus, you can just thank someone. Heard's lawyer doesn't do that. Instead, he turns it into a noun—"my thanks"—and "extends" it to them. When someone opens a door for us, we don't "extend our thanks to them." We say, "Thank you." Also, Heard's

lawyer uses the conditional mood, saying "I would like." This makes his "thank you" wordier and less confident. The conditional mood is usually used to express things that are uncertain. Sometimes we use it as a polite way to request things. But Heard's lawyer has no reason to be uncertain or hesitant about saying "thanks."

- **"on behalf of Amber and our whole legal team"**—This is an unnecessary prepositional phrase. Prepositional phrases ("on behalf of") make statements wordier and less engaging. Also, it is implied he is talking for Amber and the team, but if he wants to make that explicit, he could just say "for."
- **"the care and diligence"**—Non-lawyers don't use the phrase "care and diligence." How about "hard work"?
- **"with which you have served as jurors"**—This is another wordy and unengaging prepositional phrase. People don't talk like this in the 21st century.
- **"in this matter"**—These words are unnecessary because they are implied. What other case would he be thanking them for? Also, "case" is better than "matter."

I don't mean to criticize someone saying thank you, and this certainly did not make or break the case. But it is a good example of how lawyers often take something as simple as saying "thank you" and inject extra words to complicate it.

If it had been me, I would have dropped the thank you altogether (see Chapter 1) or said it concisely with a sincere tone and good eye contact.

EXAMPLE 2: SEAN 'DIDDY' COMBS TRIAL

In the summer of 2025, Sean 'Diddy' Combs went to trial on federal charges that he ran a racketeering and sex-trafficking conspiracy, using his business empire to unlawfully coerce women into sexual activities with threats and violence. Combs beat the racketeering charge, but the way the prosecution discussed it in the closing argument is still a great example of skillful speaking. (It also shows that strong speaking skills won't save you when the evidence falls short.)

In her closing argument, federal prosecutor Christy Slavik did what great legal speakers do—she turned legalese in the court's jury instructions into plain English. She knew her audience.

In every RICO prosecution—short for the "Racketeer Influenced and Corrupt Organizations Act"—one of the hardest things for the government to explain to jurors is what a RICO violation is.

Among other things, the instructions require the government to prove that a criminal "enterprise" existed. But when jurors hear the word "enterprise," most don't know what it means, unless you're talking about the car rental company. In her argument, Slavik clearly understood this because she gave jurors a substitute word they would all understand—"group."

She told jurors that they "may have heard the term 'racketeering' before in the context of mafia organized crime, but the concept is simple." She said, "The law recognizes that **when someone commits a crime as part of a group, what the law calls an enterprise, they're more powerful and more dangerous.**" And she said that an enterprise is "not a complicated or special thing."

In the end, she told jurors "what the evidence shows is that over and over, the defendant and his inner circle agreed to commit crimes together. That's what a racketeering conspiracy is."

This is a great example of the plain, simple language we should use—not just with jurors, but whenever we speak. Remember Slavik's translation ("enterprise" = "group") and look for similar ones the next time you present.

A Good Exercise for Jury Instructions

While jury instructions are technically written in English, most jurors don't understand them. As an advocate, your job is to put them in words jurors can understand.

A helpful exercise before any trial is to run the instructions in your case through a free readability checker. Lumos Learning offers a good one that will score your text across a variety of readability tests, including the Flesch-Kincaid and Automated Readability Index tests.

While the authors of pattern jury instructions have tried to make them readable by a wide range of people, many still fail. For example, California's pattern instruction for the basic standard of care in negligence cases gets a "C" on Lumos Learning. It is written at a high-school or early college level, which is beyond the level of many jurors.

If the instructions in your case get similar scores, think about how you can simplify them to speak to more jurors. This is also an area where pasting the instructions into an AI tool, like ChatGPT or Claude, and asking it to rewrite the instruction can help (just make sure the rewrite is legally accurate!).

Quick Tip from an Advocate

Carley Palmer is a partner at Halpern, May, Ybarra, and Gelberg—a litigation boutique in Los Angeles. She is a seasoned trial and appellate lawyer, who served for more than eight years as a federal prosecutor. I asked her for a tip about finding words that will work for any audience. This is what she said:

> Talk about your case to non-lawyers at social events. When someone asks, "What do you do?" or "What are you working on these days?" use that opportunity to practice explaining your case in a way that's understandable and pulls people in. If you get a confused or dazed look, then you'll know that's a story you can still work to tell more clearly or to paint in a more intriguing light.

9.2 Don't Be Afraid to Show Humility and Vulnerability, Sometimes

We will never win a case just because the judge or jury likes us. But having them like us doesn't hurt.

Humility and vulnerability are two things that get others to like us.[8] As one *Harvard Business Review* article says, "Only presenting an idealized version of

8. Arthur Aron et al., *The Experimental Generation of Interpersonal Closeness: A Procedure and Some Preliminary Findings*, 23 PERS. & SOC. PSYCHOL. BULL. 363 (1997).

ourselves separates us from others."[9] We don't relate to people covered in body armor. We relate to real people.

It's no coincidence that the *Official TED Guide to Public Speaking* lists vulnerability and humility as two of the five ways to connect with the audience.[10] (Eye contact, humor, and storytelling are the other three.)

Now, I don't want us to go overboard here. Exuding confidence is important for being persuasive. We don't want to be so humble that we lack confidence. And we don't want to share irrelevant personal information that hurts our image.

Instead, we want to—at times—show humility and vulnerability in a confident way. I'll give you two examples.

EXAMPLE 1: ONE OF MY MENTORS

In 2021, I tried an eight-figure real estate case with one of my senior partners. He was an experienced attorney with impressive accomplishments, but it had been more than 40 years since he graduated law school. He was rusty on the rules of evidence.

While he was examining a witness, the judge kept sustaining hearsay objections, which baffled my partner because the out-of-court statements were made by the same witness who was on the stand. He turned to me, puzzled, and I told him the judge was right; those can still be hearsay.

He let the issue go and told the judge it was "not the key to the case." (A lawyer let something go? Who's heard of that?)

He could have left it there, but the next morning before trial, he told the judge he wanted to share something. He said, "Your Honor, last night I reread the Evidence Code you kept talking about, and I'm happy to report you were right. It was all hearsay." The judge laughed, and a few months later decided the case in our favor (it was a bench trial).

She didn't decide for us because of this moment. But she liked my partner and paid attention to everything he said. I think it helped that he showed humility sometimes.

---

9. Michael Simmons, *To Create a Real Connection, Show Vulnerability*, Harv. Bus. Rev. (May 9, 2014), https://hbr.org/2014/05/to-create-a-real-connection-show-vulnerability.

10. Anderson, cited above in Chapter 3, note 20, at 55.

EXAMPLE 2: ME

This second example is from an embarrassing moment in one of my trials. I was trying a case in a busy criminal courtroom, where the counsel table was covered with papers and forms kept on it by the hardworking calendar attorneys who covered the morning pretrial cases.

I was about to address the jury for the very first time in jury selection. The judge turned to me and said, "Mr. Snow, are you ready?"

I said, "Yes, Your Honor," stood up, and immediately knocked what seemed like 1,000 pieces of paper on the floor. They scattered everywhere.

I shrugged it off and said, "Well, that's not how I practiced this last night. Let me pick all this up and try again." I didn't pretend it didn't happen. I didn't run from it. I acknowledged it was not what I wanted to happen and made a small joke out of it.

During the next break, I was shocked when my colleague asked if I planned it. I asked why. He explained, "Because they loved you in that moment. I don't think there was a better way you could have started."

I don't know if I agree with him, but it was nice to hear a positive spin on something embarrassing. The lesson I learned was, if you are nice to those around you, they will root for you to succeed, even when you stumble.

In every trial, moments come when things don't go as planned. Don't let it discourage you. Owning those small moments will show you are a real person, and that helps in the end.

Amazingly, research suggests that small blunders—like me knocking over the papers—can make some people *more* persuasive to the audience. Psychologists call it the "pratfall effect." The effect was first studied by Elliot Aronson (from Chapter 2) in the 1960s. He found that highly competent people were perceived to be more likable, and thus persuasive, if they committed a small blunder in front of the audience, like spilling coffee on themselves.[11] The theory is that the audience often perceives highly competent people (such as lawyers) to be superior, and making a small mistake humanizes them, causing the audience to like them more. (Note: It only worked for people the audience already saw as competent; for those viewed as average, the blunders made

11. Elliot Aronson, et al., *The Effect of a Pratfall on Increasing Interpersonal Attractiveness*, 4 Psychonomic Sci. 227 (1966).

them less likable. And unfortunately, men benefit from the effect more than women, which my wife intuited the moment I told her about it.)

While we're at it, it's also okay to be nice to the other side and acknowledge when they do a good job. This should not be contrived, but when others see it, they will also like you more.

Equally important is not being too proud or arrogant. Avoid name-dropping, telling stories just to show off, or boasting about achievements. If we talk only about ourselves, it's only a matter of time before the audience tunes out.

Sometimes we get so caught up in playing the part of a lawyer that we lose some of our humanity. We need to bring it back.

Quick Tip from an Advocate

Martin Estrada is a partner at Munger, Tolles & Olson, and previously served as the United States Attorney for the Central District of California. I asked him for a tip about becoming a better speaker. This is what he said:

> Be yourself. This may sound trite, but too many people make the mistake of trying to act or sound like how they think a trial lawyer should behave. Presenting as your authentic self will achieve at least three critical goals: first, the audience will view you as being more sincere; second, the audience will feel they know you and therefore better connect with your points and arguments; and third, you will eliminate the added stress of trying to act out a role that isn't really you.

10

Rule Ten: Being Natural Doesn't Mean Don't Practice

Some people say they don't want to practice because they want to appear natural. This is a mistake. It will backfire.

Every impressive, natural-looking speaker practices intensely.

Many TED speakers rehearse 100 hours or more for an 18-minute presentation. Dr. Jill Bolte Taylor, a Harvard-trained neuroanatomist and TED speaker with more than 20 million views, rehearsed 200 times to achieve the "conversational" delivery in her hit talk.[1]

Stand-up comedians like Jerry Seinfeld workshop their material on stage for months, if not years, before putting it in their TV specials.

Steve Jobs practiced his keynotes until he knew them cold, and then he kept practicing.[2]

It is well-known that former President Obama practiced extensively before giving a big speech.[3]

---

1. Carmine Gallo, *The Best TED Speakers Practice This 1 Habit Before Taking the Stage*, Inc.com (May 7, 2017), https://www.inc.com/carmine-gallo/the-best-ted-speakers-practice-this-1-habit-before-taking-the-stage.html.

2. Jason Aten, *Steve Jobs's Masterful Presentation Ability Came Down to 1 Underrated Thing. Anyone Can Do It*, Inc.com (Feb. 24, 2023), https://www.inc.com/jason-aten/steve-jobs-masterful-presentation-ability-came-down-to-1-underrated-thing-anyone-can-do-it.html.

3. Sein Beilock, Choke: What the Secrets of the Brain Reveal About Getting It Right When You Have To 443 (2011).

Mark Twain said, "It usually takes me more than three weeks to prepare a good impromptu speech."

Media trainer Bill McGowan says, "No one graduates from eloquence school"—"[e]ven accomplished public speakers must continue to prepare just as diligently and rehearse just as thoroughly as they did when they were less experienced."[4]

I could keep going.

The irony is that rehearsing is what makes us look "natural." If we don't rehearse, we won't look natural.

When we say a speaker is "natural," what we actually mean is that they have smooth delivery. They always know what to say next. They never search for a forgotten point in their notes. They're present the entire time. They know their material so well the speech doesn't seem planned. It seems like they are just speaking the truth.

These speakers achieve this only with lots and lots of practice. As we discussed last chapter, many of us have natural behaviors that make us look uncomfortable on stage, like touching our face or looking around too much. We need to practice so we can eliminate them and look more confident and natural.

Trial advocacy trainers Brian Johnson and Marsha Hunter call this the "Paradox of Naturalness." They say, "As an advocate you need to consciously employ certain *unnatural* behaviors to look and feel *natural*."[5] And the only way to get good at the unnatural behaviors is to practice them.

Body language expert Mark Bowden gave an excellent TEDx Talk on "The Importance of Being Inauthentic" when public speaking. He told his audience, "If I was being truly authentic with you, I would not show up for this" because "the last thing I want to do at an instinctual gut level is to stand in front of a bunch of people who I don't know ... and put out there my life's work for them to criticize."[6]

He said that if he acts authentically and honestly then "you're not going to listen to me." But because he wants people to listen, he chooses his behaviors carefully. He acts and performs as their friend. He doesn't trust his natural instincts. He plans and rehearses his delivery.

---

4. McGowan, cited above in Chapter 1, note 6, at 32.

5. Johnson & Hunter, cited above in Chapter 5, note 5, at 2.

6. Mark Bowden, *The Importance of Being Authentic*, TEDxTORONTO (Oct. 22, 2013), https://www.youtube.com/watch?v=1zpf8H_Dd40.

This advice should resonate with anyone who fears public speaking. According to Mark Twain, that is all of us. He said, "There are two types of speakers: those that are nervous and those that are liars."

We need to psych ourselves up to talk in front of an audience. Our true, authentic selves don't want to be there. We need practice to get in the right state of mind.

This means standing up and doing it out loud at full volume. Sitting down and softly mumbling it to ourselves doesn't work.

Do you think actors and singers do that when rehearsing for a performance? We are no less a performer than they are, so we should practice the same way.

Speaking is a physical act that involves our whole body. Thus, practicing out loud also builds muscle memory, guaranteeing that each extra time we do it will be smoother—just like athletes and musicians.

Research shows this type of deliberate practice is the most effective. Dr. Sian Beilock is a cognitive scientist and one of the world's foremost experts on performance under pressure. (She is also the President of Dartmouth College.) Her research shows that the best way to ensure strong performance is to practice under pressure, and even mild levels of stress make a big difference. This applies to everyone from top athletes to police officers in high-stakes confrontations, to high school test takers, to public speakers.

She writes, "Simulating low levels of stress helps prevent cracking under increased pressure, because people who practice this way learn to stay calm, cool, and collected in the face of whatever comes their way."[7] For public speakers, "[g]etting used to the pressure of speaking in front of others helps people not react as negatively in the future ... [and] makes public speaking a lot less daunting."[8]

So we should practice in front of other people, if we can. Even rehearsing before a close friend, loved one, or colleague can add the low levels of stress needed to prepare our nerves for the big moment. Practicing in front of a camera—knowing we plan to watch it later—can also simulate the stress of speaking to others. As business communication expert Carmine Gallo says, "A comfortable performance doesn't happen without hours and hours of practice—preferably in front of an audience."[9]

---

7. BEILOCK, cited above in note 3, at 77.

8. *Id.* at 443.

9. Carmine Gallo, cited above in note 1.

Rehearsing out loud doesn't just prepare our nerves; it is also an indispensable part of the editing process. Only after we stand up and practice the words out loud do we discover if they sound good to the ear. Or whether the sentences we planned are awkward to say. Or when we should pause and for how long. Or when we should speak louder or lower our voice.

Would we ever turn in the first draft of a brief without printing it out, reading it, and editing it? Never. Great writers know that editing is where the magic happens—where adequate briefs become excellent ones.

When we give a speech without rehearsing, it's like turning in our very first, roughest draft. We lose all the improvement available from simply watching ourselves perform a few times and tweaking the parts that don't sound right.

Confessions of a Public Speaker author Scott Berkun says he practices so he can "safely make dozens of mistakes and correct them before anyone ever sees it. It's possible I'm not a better public speaker than anyone else—I'm just better at catching and fixing problems."[10]

Watching ourselves can be painful. That's why we don't do it. It's also the most painful when we are new to public speaking, which unfortunately leads to early experiences that are so traumatic we write them off entirely. But we need to work through this. I promise light is at the end of the tunnel. The more we watch ourselves, the more we get used to the way we look and sound to others. It's scientifically proven to work. Psychologists call it the "mere exposure" effect. We prefer things that we are more familiar with, and the more often we are exposed to something, the more we prefer it. So we need to suspend our cringe reflex and watch the tape. Once we get familiar with how we look and sound on camera, it will only get easier.

In short, once we've carved out the time to practice, don't do it halfheartedly. We need to do it on our feet, out loud, and in an environment that simulates the real day. And we need to record it and watch the tape. This is the only way we can guarantee the audience gets the best speech inside us, and that we don't regret our performance on game day.

10. Scott Berkun, *Confessions of a Public Speaker*, https://scottberkun.com/speaking-fear/ (last visited Apr. 30, 2025).

EXAMPLE: *UNITED STATES V. BUCK*

This last example comes from one of the best trial attorneys I know, who is an expert preparer and never regrets her performance on game day. She also happens to be my wife, Chelsea Norell.

I'm lucky to be married to a federal prosecutor who has tried over a dozen cases, including high-profile ones in the news. One reason I'm lucky is that I get to witness the behind-the-scenes work that goes into her trials. I know that the reason she succeeds—on top of being smart—is that she puts in the work.

For every trial, Chelsea practices her opening statements and closing arguments on her feet, out loud, and in front of other people. Her office's custom has their attorneys do mock openings and closings before trial—but she goes beyond that. She practices it for me, her mom, and anyone else who will listen. It shows in the final work product.

In 2021, she tried a criminal case against a wealthy political donor whose fetish was to lure vulnerable men—often homeless—to his apartment and inject them with methamphetamine in exchange for money. He killed two in the process and was charged with distribution of methamphetamine resulting in death, human trafficking, and maintaining a drug premises. The case was a big deal in Los Angeles and inspired later episodes of Law & Order and Bosch: Legacy.

Her courtroom arguments were often quoted in the news, but what stood out most to me was her rebuttal argument at the end of the case. In criminal cases, the prosecution gives a rebuttal argument to respond to what the defense says in its closing, and the prosecution never knows exactly what they are going to say. Because rebuttals are given on the spot, many are rushed and slightly disorganized.

Not my Chelsea's. Hers was a highlight of the trial and made the news.[11] It was smooth, crisply worded, and engaged the jury with rhetorical questions and vivid imagery.

For example, the defense's closing attacked the living victims that testified, calling them opportunistic men who chose to inject drugs and were

---

11. Hailey Branson-Potts & Michael Finnegan, *Ed Buck's Defense Accused of 'Despicable Victim Shaming' in Fatal Meth Overdose Trial*, L.A. Times (July 23, 2021), https://www.latimes.com/california/story/2021-07-23/ed-buck-federal-methamphetamine-trial.

now seeking fame and attention by testifying at the public trial. Here are two things she said to respond to that.

First:

> When the choice is to take another slam or walk home in the middle of the night from West Hollywood back to Compton, is that a meaningful choice? When the choice is to slam or sleep in a homeless encampment in the Devil's Dips, is that a meaningful choice? It's easy to talk about choices when you have lots of good ones. But Buck specifically targeted people who did not have a lot of good choices.

Second:

> [Defense counsel] said that these victims just wanted their 15 minutes of fame. [But] is this something you'd want to be famous for? Or is this a horrifying thing to have to go through? Did those witnesses look like they wanted to be talking to you, telling these deeply personal humiliating experiences to you? [Three of them wept at trial.]

When you read these passages, pay attention to the rhythm of the words. Take note of the parallel structure she uses in the first two sentences in the first example. Look at the specific images she conjures—like walking across the city in the middle of the night or sleeping in the "Devil's Dips" (a dangerous urban watershed area in Los Angeles). Notice the lack of filler words. See how she uses plain words and short, easy sentences.

This doesn't read like a rebuttal transcript—it reads like a well-prepared and thought-out argument. And the secret is that most of it was. While Chelsea didn't know exactly what the defense attorney would say in closing, she had a good enough idea to prepare for it. So that's what she did.

I asked her for a quote about preparation and here is what she says:

> I prepare so I can maximize my autopilot at trial. The structure of my argument, themes, certain turns of phrase—I plot and practice that so that when I'm in court, I can devote all my brain power to listening and responding to the unexpected.

This is a great lesson for all of us. The best speakers prepare so they can focus their mental energy on being in the moment. That's how they appear natural.

Quick Tip from an Appellate Advocate

Stefan Love is a partner at Greines, Martin Stein & Richland LLP—an appellate litigation boutique in Los Angeles. He has argued appeals in the California Supreme Court, the California Court of Appeals, and the Ninth Circuit. I asked him for a tip about preparing for oral argument. This is what he said:

> Here is the most efficient method I know to prepare for any presentation to a court—from a motion hearing to an appellate argument.
>
> First, break up your presentation into discrete "talking points." A talking point could be a factual/record detail, a legal standard, an analogy or distinction with an on-point case, an answer to a likely tough question—anything that might come up. There might be 2 to 3 points for a hearing, and 20+ points for an appellate argument.
>
> Second, use index cards to practice your talking points. On one side of each card, write a prompt for the point (e.g., "standard of review"; "distinguish *Smith*"; etc.). Then—the most important part—practice talking through the point *aloud*, *exactly* as though you were talking to a court.
>
> Use a stopwatch. Each point should take no more than two minutes to say aloud. The first several times you talk through a point, it will be awkward and too long. Still, *don't* write down what you're going to say word-for-word. Force yourself to develop and refine the point orally. You'll be much more fluent and confident at the argument as a result."

Quick Tip for Job Interviews

Another benefit of practicing your speaking skills is that it gives you something interesting to talk about in job interviews.

One question I always hated getting in interviews was, "What's your biggest weakness?" It feels like a trap, and it's hard to give an authentic answer. The conventional wisdom says to respond with a weakness that is really a strength, but that makes the answer sound contrived, not genuine.

My tip for answering this question (which interviewers should stop asking) is this: instead of responding with a weakness, respond with something you're currently working on, like public speaking.

"What's your biggest weakness?" "Well, right now I'm working on my public speaking [or insert whatever else it is: using AI to be more efficient, promoting yourself more, networking, etc.]."

Then immediately start talking about all the things you are doing to get better and how you're enjoying them, like reading books, going to Toastmasters meetings, doing stand-up comedy at night, etc. The interviewer's follow-up questions will likely focus on these things rather than your personal shortcomings.

This also avoids conceding a weakness and shows you're a curious person who is proactive about getting better. Yes, you've technically dodged the question, but the interviewer doesn't actually care about your self-diagnosed weaknesses. They want to see how you think and learn who you are.

It's much better to be seen as someone who is always growing than someone with a weakness they are doing nothing about.

OTHER CONSIDERATIONS

11

What About Stories?

"Tell a story."

This is common advice in many public speaking books. Why don't I have it as a rule? Because it's not specific or original enough to be as helpful as the other rules. And ten rules sound better than eleven.

Still, it is good advice. I agree with it. We should tell stories—lots of them.

Stories are one of the best ways to connect with the audience and persuade them. As a species, we are hardwired for stories. We've used them for 150,000 years to connect with others and learn how to organize our lives.[1] We know how to follow them starting in early childhood. They are easy for our brains to process. Some people say they are the whole reason we developed language.

As the late trial advocacy professor Jim McElhaney writes:

> Since long before the start of recorded history, stories are what people have used to learn, to teach, to understand how the world works, to grapple with moral principles, to memorialize events. In fact, people are typically able to understand far more difficult ideas and situations through stories than they could ever grasp through dry abstractions.[2]

---

1. Kendall Haven, *Your Brain on Story*, Stanford mediaX Seminar (Mar. 30, 2015), https://www.youtube.com/watch?v=zGrf0LGn6Y4; Kendall Haven, Story Proof: The Science Behind the Startling Power of Story 3–4 (2007).

2. James W. McElhaney, *Balanced Persuasion*, A.B.A. J., Mar. 2002.

Modern science reveals that stories connect us at the neuron level. In studies, brain scans have shown that when we tell a story, the audience's brain waves start to synchronize with ours.[3]

Other research suggests that packaging a message in a story reduces the audience's resistance to it.[4] Many people are skeptical of new information. When a speaker presents a new idea, the audience internally counterargues with it, almost immediately. They test it against what they know and look for holes before accepting it. But because stories draw us into storylines and characters, they disarm this natural skepticism. We get so wrapped up in the story that we stop counterarguing.

In short, stories bring many advantages. They are how we should present most of our information.

So how do we tell good stories that engage the audience?

We follow the 10 rules in this book. We use tension and release to make them not boring (Chapter 1). We frame them with things the audience cares about (Chapter 2). We use simple words and relatable concepts that make it easy for the audience to follow and understand (Chapters 3–5). We add pictures (Chapter 6). We tell them with an engaging voice and body language (Chapters 7–8). We act like a real person (Chapter 9). And we practice (Chapter 10).

Many of the lawyers cited in this book used storytelling—from Justice Ginsburg to John Hueston to Camille Vasquez to Ted Olson to Justice Sotomayor.

One cannot be a great trial lawyer without being a great storyteller. This means we need to tell lots of stories. We can treat it as a rule if we want.

---

3. Greg J. Stephens, Lauren J. Silbert & Uri Hasson, *Speaker–Listener Neural Coupling Underlies Successful Communication*, 107 Proc. Nat'l Acad. Sci. 14425 (2010).

4. Chelsea L. Ratcliff & Ye Sun, *Overcoming Resistance Through Narratives: Findings from a Meta-Analytic Review*, 46 Hum. Comm. Res. 345 (2020).

12

The Dreaded Nerves

Ah, the dreaded nerves. Most public speaking books start here, with advice about overcoming your fear of public speaking.

I chose not to.

I don't even have a rule about it.

I just don't think it's a good place to devote our mental energy, and it is highly individual.

We should instead focus on our content and techniques.

Plus, something remarkable happens when we've honed the perfect presentation—one with content that's been carefully crafted for our specific audience and that we've rehearsed enough to remove the kinks. Our nerves fade. They don't go away entirely. But we're more confident and more excited for the moment because we've put in the work.

Calmness is a by-product of our practice and preparation.

John Wooden had a similar philosophy for coaching basketball. He never focused on winning. Allegedly, he never even uttered the word. He thought that "when you start fixating on winning, you lose sight of doing your job."

Instead, he encouraged his players to put in their best effort every day, and to strive to be the best version of themselves.

In his book *Wooden on Leadership*, he writes:

> For most of my life I have believed that success is found in the running of the race. How you run the race—your planning, preparation, practice, and performance—counts for everything. Winning or losing is a by-product, and aftereffect, of that effort. For me, it's the quality of your

efforts that counts most and offers the greatest and most long-lasting satisfaction.[1]

Let's carry this over to speaking. In the weeks before your talk, don't think about your nerves on game day. It's hard to control your nerves in advance. Instead, focus on planning, preparing, and practicing the best presentation you can. Following the rules in this book will help. When game day comes, you will feel less nervous knowing you have something great to give the audience instead of something mediocre.

This fits with the research of Dr. Beilock—the expert on performance under pressure we discussed in Chapter 10. In her TED talk, *Why We Choke Under Pressure—And How to Avoid It*, she says:

> We often get in our own way precisely because our worries prompt us to concentrate too much.... [W]e pay too much attention to what we're doing. When we're concerned about performing our best, we often try and control aspects of what we're doing that are best left on autopilot, outside conscious awareness, and as a result, we mess up.[2]

Focusing on our nerves can do more harm than good—it can make our nervousness a self-fulfilling prophecy. Focus on the material instead.

But if that's not enough, here are other things that could help (and they're all better than imagining the audience naked):

- **Practice, practice, practice**—Reread Chapter 10. Practicing deliberately and under low levels of stress can help reduce your nerves at the actual event. And even when you don't have a speaking event or trial scheduled, try to speak in public whenever you get the chance. This will get you more familiar with the experience and help you reduce your nerves the next time you do have an important speaking event. Think of it as a form of "exposure therapy," which studies have shown to be effective in treating social anxiety disorder, post-traumatic stress disorder, and various phobias. I list this method first because it's helped me the most in my speaking.

---

1. John Wooden, Wooden on Leadership 33 (2005).

2. Sian Leah Beilock, *Why We Choke Under Pressure—and How to Avoid It*, TED (Nov. 2017), https://www.ted.com/talks/sian_leah_beilock_why_we_choke_under_pressure_and_how_to_avoid_it/.

- **Know your beginning cold**—Having confidence at the beginning of your presentation can carry over to the rest of it. But faltering out of the gates can add to your nerves and make it harder to recover.
- **Think more about your audience**—You can reduce your anxiety by getting out of your head and focusing on the audience and their needs. Many therapists give this same advice to shy people—stop thinking about yourself so much and think about the other person. Your audience wants you to succeed. They don't want you to be a nervous mess. If you fill your brain with thinking about what they want, there's no room to worry about yourself.
- **Reframe your nerves as excitement**—Alison Wood Brooks, a Harvard Business School professor with a Ph.D. in Decision Processes, did several studies involving public speaking and karaoke to see if people could reframe their anxiety as excitement.[3] The answer was yes. Those who did it also performed better than those who tried to calm their nerves. All it entailed was saying "I am excited" before their task.

  In her paper, Wood Brooks writes, "Compared with reappraising anxiety as calmness or not reappraising anxiety at all, reappraising anxiety as excitement increased the subjective experience of excitement and improved performance in … public speaking" as well as karaoke (if you care about that). She also states that the more a person uses positive self-talk, the more it works, creating an "upward spiral." This finding is generally consistent with the research underlying "cognitive behavioral therapy" (CBT) that says we can use our words, thoughts, and behaviors to change how we feel. If you are unfamiliar with CBT, it is worth reading more about.
- **Hold a power pose**—Many people recommend holding a "power pose" or "superhero pose"—standing tall with your shoulders back and feet firmly planted—to induce feelings of self-confidence. Some research suggests they work,[4] and it led to one of the most viewed TED Talks of all time by one of the researchers, psychologist Amy Cuddy. Since then, other researchers have had problems replicating the re-

3. A.W. Brooks, *Get Excited: Reappraising Pre-Performance Anxiety as Excitement*, 143 J. Experimental Psych.: Gen. 1144 (2014).

4. Dana R. Carney, Amy J.C. Cuddy & Andy J. Yap, *Power Posing: Brief Nonverbal Displays Affect Neuroendocrine Levels and Risk Tolerance*, 21 Psychol. Sci. 1363 (2010).

sults[5] and one of Cuddy's co-authors no longer thinks the power-pose effects are real.[6] Still, I haven't seen anything saying these are harmful, so they are good to use if they help you feel more confident.

- **Burn off adrenaline with a quick exercise**—Our bodies produce adrenaline before stressful events to prepare us for a fight or flight. But we shouldn't be fighting or fleeing when we present to an audience, so this adrenaline is unhelpful. Research tells us that quick cardiovascular exercises—like jumping jacks or pushups—help our bodies process adrenaline and return to a state of calm. So if your heart is racing and your hands are shaking before a speech, try a quick cardio exercise to reduce those adrenaline jitters.

In the end, most of us cannot quell our nerves entirely. Even the King of Rock and Roll—Elvis Presley—went through stage fright before every show. Thus, communications coach Matt Abrahams says, "The goal isn't to eradicate anxiety but rather to prevent it from hampering us."[7]

We can't take a magic pill—at least not one I can prescribe. We need to put in the work and practice our speaking on a regular basis. The best time to start is now.

5. Eva Ranehill, et al., *Assessing the Robustness of Power Posing: No Effect on Hormones and Risk Tolerance in a Large Sample of Men and Women*, 26 Psychol. Sci. 653 (2015).

6. Maquita Peters, 'Power Poses' Co-Author: 'I Do Not Believe The Effects Are Real', NPR (Oct. 1, 2016), https://www.npr.org/2016/10/01/496093672/power-poses-co-author-i-do-not-believe-the-effects-are-real.

7. Matt Abrahams, Think Faster Talk Smarter: How to Speak Successfully When You're Put on the Spot 30 (2023).

13

Crave Feedback

Some people have a hard time hearing feedback. Don't be one of them. Constructive—or even negative—feedback is not a judgment of your character; it's another person's assessment of your skills in that moment. Most of the time, it comes from a good place. And when you are new to something, no one expects your skills to be great.

You should crave feedback because it accelerates your growth. Early in your career, many people will give you free feedback—professors, colleagues, senior attorneys, and mentors. Take it. Listen closely to it. And thank them for it. As attorneys get deeper into their careers, they pay lots of money for feedback from professional coaches and consultants.

Some of this feedback will include bad advice and inaccurate observations. That's okay. Treat it as a small datapoint. If you seek feedback from different sources, it will be easier to decipher which feedback is true and helpful, and which isn't.

The most helpful feedback is specific. It identifies things that are, and are not, working for you. And it tells you how to fix what's not working. The trick to being good at receiving feedback is listening closely and asking for specifics. A good response to feedback goes like this: "Thank you so much. Can you give me a specific example (or demonstration) of how you would have done ________?"

Or like this: "Was this something you struggled with? How did you get better?"

It's also a good idea to ask for the rationale behind the proposed fix to help you understand the reason for doing it differently. Something like, "Thank you so much. Can you tell me more about how you landed on that approach?" (This can also help you determine whether the advice is good.)

A bad response to feedback is defensive. Rather than being curious about how to improve, the defensive response immediately explains to the person giving feedback what you were thinking and why you did what you did. It doesn't make the person giving feedback feel good or listened to. And it makes them less inclined to help you. When you're trying to build a mentoring relationship, you want to keep the conversation going, not kill it.

Giving feedback is an art too. Some people are bad at it. Ideally, the person giving feedback will also identify something you did well to encourage you. And they will focus on things you can actually fix. If you don't feel supported by the person, it's OK not to go back to them. But if you can handle it, take feedback from anyone willing to give it.

Many excellent books have been written about feedback, if you want to do a deeper dive. I recommend "Feedback Loops" by University of Michigan Law Professor Patrick Barry.

14

Exercises

14.1 Create an Attention-Grabbing Opening Line
14.2 Give a Five-to-Ten-Minute Informative Talk
14.3 Put Yourself in the Shoes of an Attorney from a Famous Case
14.4 Make an Impromptu Argument Without Filler Words
14.5 Practice Framing Tricky Issues
14.6 Practice Vocal Variety by Talking About Something You Know
14.7 Evaluate Others

Reading about speaking skills gets us only so far. Speaking is a physical act. Like other physical acts, we need to do it—repeatedly—to get better at it.

The beauty is that it works. Through consistent and deliberate practice, speakers can build good habits and muscle memory the same way top-tier athletes do. And having a solid foundation will help us perform in the moment, no matter the stakes or surprises that may be thrown at us.

This is the mindset of Stephen Curry—the greatest NBA shooter of all time. Even though he's already won that title, Curry still takes 500 practice shots every day. He says, "The reason you practice and work on it so much is that during the game, your instincts take over to a point where it feels weird if you don't do it the right way."

Here are exercises to practice the skills in this book.

14.1 Give an Attention-Grabbing Opening Line

For this exercise, find an online video of an opening statement, closing argument, or CLE presentation where the attorney did not do a good job of grabbing attention at the outset. Then come up with a better way to do it.

These videos will not be hard to find. But if you are having trouble, here are a few high-profile ones you can choose from:

- The prosecution opening statement from the first trial in *Massachusetts v. Karen Read* (2024), available at https://www.youtube.com/watch?v=8J7P4aXKGkc
- The prosecution closing argument from *People v. Conrad Murray* (2011), available at https://www.courttv.com/title/81-ca-v-murray-prosecution-closing-argument/
- The prosecution closing argument in *Tennessee v. Megan Boswell* (2025), available at https://www.youtube.com/watch?v=hFcV_81OxIM
- The prosecution closing argument in *Wisconsin v. Jennifer Crumbley* (2024), available at https://www.youtube.com/watch?v=OmqISCVio-s

You do not need to be familiar with the entire case or subject to complete this exercise. Just watch the first 5–10 minutes of the video to find content that you think would make a better grabber than the "thank yous" and lackluster procedural explanations these attorneys started with. Then film yourself giving that attention-grabbing opening. When you give it, pay special attention to how you use your voice, pauses, and body language to create a memorable moment.

14.2 Give a Five-to-Ten-Minute Informative Talk

The goal of this exercise is to take a discrete concept and prepare a five-to-ten-minute informative talk about it, trying to incorporate as many of this book's rules as you can. Pretend your audience is a group of colleagues who have come to learn from you at a continuing legal education lecture.

Because the goal is to practice your structure and delivery, choose a topic that won't require extensive research and that can be covered in 10 minutes or less. Here are a few options:

- A United States Supreme Court case scheduled to be decided in the current or upcoming term. SCOTUSblog.com is an excellent resource for information about these cases. In your presentation, discuss the issue the Court has taken up, the arguments on both sides, the potential implications of the ruling going forward, and why the audience should care about it
- A pattern jury instruction from your jurisdiction on a concept such as negligence, fraud, murder, circumstantial evidence, reasonable doubt, or the preponderance of evidence
- A discrete exception to the hearsay rule, such as party admissions, excited utterances, or business records
- A law-adjacent topic such as DNA evidence, problems with eyewitness testimony, how human memory works, fingerprint analysis, or how the body processes alcohol
- One of the public speaking rules from this book
- An advanced legal writing lesson for practitioners. Good resources for advanced legal writing tips include *Plain English for Lawyers* by Richard C. Wydick and Amy E. Sloan, *Point Made* by Ross Guberman, *Legal Writing in Plain English* by Bryan Garner, and *Elegant Legal Writing* by Ryan McCarl

Once you've picked your topic, set a timer and spend 30 minutes designing your talk, thinking about:

1. How you will open,
2. How you will use knowledge gaps to keep the audience interested,
3. How you will make it relevant to the audience,
4. What your through line or take-home message will be,
5. How you will use visuals (plan for no more than three), and
6. How you will use your voice and body language.

Don't spend more than 30 minutes on this. As attorneys, we often spend more time planning than practicing our delivery, so the timer in this drill makes sure you get to the practice stage.

Once the timer goes off, put your pencil down or close your computer and go on a two-minute walk. Then come back and film yourself giving the speech, making sure you talk for at least 5 minutes and no more than 10 minutes.

Watch the video and note what you like and what you don't. Take a 5-minute break and then film yourself giving the speech one more time. When you watch it, make a list of everything that improved.

14.3 Put Yourself in the Shoes of an Attorney from a Famous Case

The goal of this next exercise is to practice your vocal delivery and body language.

First, find a two-minute segment of an opening statement or closing argument that you think is well structured. You can use the excerpt below from prosecutor Jerry Blackwell's opening statement in the George Floyd murder trial or find another example. Videos from law school mock trial competitions are also a good source.

Second, reduce the excerpt to a series of short bullet points that you can remember, so you aren't reading from a script when you give it.

Third, film yourself giving the statement as if you were presenting it to a jury. Assume the court does not require you to stay at the lectern the entire time.

Fourth, watch the tape. When you watch it, note the following: (1) how many times you pause in the first minute, (2) how long your pauses are, (3) how many words you say in the first minute, (4) how many hand gestures you use, and (5) how much variety is in your voice.

Then compare these to the best speakers, remembering that they:

- often have 10 pauses of 1 second or longer for every minute of speaking time,
- speak between 120–170 words per minute,
- use 20+ hand gestures per minute, and
- have lots of vocal variety

If you have a computer with Microsoft PowerPoint, use the "Rehearse with Coach" feature when you practice so it can keep track of many of these stats for you (*see* Chapter 7.1 for more information on "Rehearse with Coach").

Excerpt from Jerry Blackwell's Opening Statement in George Floyd Murder Trial:

> You're going to learn in this case a lot about what it means to be a public servant and to have the honor of wearing this badge. It's a small badge that carries with it a large responsibility and a large accountability to the public. What does it stand for? It represents the very motto of the Minneapolis Police Department, to protect with courage, to serve with compassion, but it also represents the essence of the Minneapolis Police Department approach to the use of force against its citizens when appropriate. The sanctity of life and the protection of the public shall be the cornerstones of the Minneapolis Police Department's use of force. Compassion, sanctity of life are cornerstones and that little badge is worn right over the officer's heart.
>
> But you're also going to learn that the officers take an oath when they become police officers. They take an oath that I will enforce the law courteously and appropriately. And as you will learn as it applies to this case, never employing unnecessary force or violence. And not only that, I recognize the badge of my office as a symbol of public faith and I accept it as a public trust to be held so long as I am true to the ethics of police service.
>
> Symbol of public faith, ethics to police service, sanctity of life, all of this matters tremendously to this case because you will learn that on May 25th of 2020, Mr. Derek Chauvin betrayed this badge when he used excessive and unreasonable force upon the body of Mr. George Floyd, that he put his knees upon his neck and his back grinding and crushing him until the very breath, no ladies and gentlemen, until the very life was squeezed out of him. You will learn that he was well aware that Mr. Floyd was unarmed, that Mr. Floyd had not threatened anyone, that Mr. Floyd was in handcuffs, he was completely in the control of the police, he was defenseless.

14.4 Make an Impromptu Argument Without Filler Words

Attorneys also need to speak well extemporaneously (meaning on their feet). Whether responding to an unanticipated question at oral argument, at the end of a CLE, or on a client call, attorneys cannot afford to waver in their responses, substantively or stylistically. Speaking smoothly and decisively in these situations will help you achieve your goal. That might be persuading a judge to decide for your client, establishing your true expertise in a room full of colleagues, or getting a potential client to hire you.

To practice this skill, pick one of the debate topics below, take a position on it, and give a two-minute argument in support of your position with no prep time. Your argument should clearly state what your position is and support it with 2–3 reasons. On top of that, aim to use no filler words. To keep yourself honest, record the argument and play it back to see how you did.

Debate topics

1. Should law schools ban students using AI?
2. Should Supreme Court Justices have term limits instead of lifetime appointments?
3. Should lawyers use one or two spaces after a period?
4. Should law school be two years instead of three?
5. Is it ethical to defend a client you know is guilty of a crime?
6. Is a hot dog a sandwich?
7. Is cereal soup?
8. Should access to the internet be a constitutional right?
9. Should all law firms allow telework?
10. Should Crocs (the shoes) be allowed in the office?

14.5 Practice Framing Tricky Issues

Chapter 2.2 discussed framing as an important skill for lawyers. Recall how Ted Olson framed his support of same-sex marriage around conservative values in his Newsweek article explaining why he joined the Proposition 8 case. Or how John Hueston avoided talking about his client's wealth to better appeal to everyday jurors in his counterfeit wine case. The goal of this exercise is to help you develop the same skill.

For this exercise, take one of the following debate topics (repeated from above), but this time come up with 3–5 bullet points for how you will strategically argue the position to the audience member listed in the prompt.

1. Your law school's biggest donor is the CEO of a large AI company. Write 3–5 bullet points to support an argument to this person that the school should ban the use of AI by its students.
2. There is currently a 6–3 conservative majority on the Supreme Court. Write 3–5 bullet points to support an argument to a conservative senator that they should support a bill putting term limits on Supreme Court justices. (Or the alternative: 3–5 bullet points to support an argument to a liberal senator that they should not support a bill putting term limits on Justices.)
3. Your firm's managing partner is a traditionalist who has used two spaces after a period since law school. Write 3–5 bullet points to support an argument to them that they should use one space after a period.
4. You are talking to a law school professor who teaches upper-level courses and supports themselves entirely with their law school salary. Write 3–5 bullet points to support an argument to them that law school should be two years and not three.
5. You are talking to someone who has been the victim of a mugging, a home burglary, and a hit and run. Write 3–5 bullet points to support an argument to them that it is ethical for a lawyer to defend someone they know is guilty of a crime.
6. You are talking to a senior law firm partner who spent their entire career working in the office and sees it as a good way to build office culture. Write 3–5 bullet points to support an argument to them that the firm should adopt a flexible telework policy.
7. You are talking to a senior law firm partner who wears a suit and tie to the office every day. Write 3–5 bullet points to support an argument to them that Crocs (the shoes) should be allowed in the office.

14.6 Practice Vocal Variety by Talking About Something You Know

This exercise forces you to practice vocal variety by talking about something you know so well that you don't need to think about it and can instead focus completely on the delivery.

To do it, take something you know by heart—like the moment you decided to go to law school, describing your morning commute, or even reciting the ABCs or counting to 20—and deliver it in the most interesting way possible. Build in 3 or 4 dramatic pauses, bring your voice down to a whisper for a moment, and talk at different speeds, volumes, and pitches. Remember to also use hand gestures and avoid filler.

The exercise may feel silly at first, but don't let that deter you. By cutting off your brain's need to think about the words, the exercise will let you home in on your vocal delivery like never before. The goal is to get outside your comfort zone so you can develop new ways of speaking that will eventually feel natural to you. Reread the discussion of the Law of Opposites in Chapter 7.2. If you find yourself talking mostly in one way during this drill (fast, slow, loud, quiet, etc.), try immediately doing the opposite.

14.7 Evaluate Others

Professional sports teams watch lots of game tape because it helps them identify strengths and weaknesses in themselves and their opponents.

Basketball players, especially, spend hours watching their competition so they can steal their moves. For example, NBA-newcomer Brandon Boston Jr. told ESPN that he repeatedly watched highlight videos of All-Star Paul George to memorize his crossovers, hesitations, and other moves.[1] So did 2023 number two pick Brandon Miller. He browsed YouTube for Paul George videos because George was the player whose moves he wanted to steal.

As speakers, we should adopt this approach. In this exercise, watch some attorney speeches on YouTube—or better yet, in court—and score them using the scorecard below. Videos from law school mock trial competitions are great sources too, particularly the final rounds. Believe it or not, many of these are better than videos of real attorneys.

Use the scorecard's right-hand column to take notes about techniques you particularly liked that you might try in your next speech. And to give yourself more practice speaking, film yourself giving a three-to-five-minute critique based on the information in your notes.

1. Ohm Youngmisuk, *Paul George Is the Model for a New Generation of NBA Players and NBA 2K Gamers Alike*, ESPN (Mar. 26, 2024), https://www.espn.com/nba/story/_/id/39809501/paul-george-archetype-nba-next-generation.

Speech Evaluation Scorecard

Component	Score (1–5)	Notes
Did the intro grab your attention?		
Did the speaker maintain your attention throughout? How?		
Did they make it about the jurors? How?		
Did they frame their argument strategically? How so?		
Did they emphasize effective facts and details?		
Did they have a strong though line?		
Were their points easy to understand? Did they use strong analogies?		
Did they avoid verbal clutter?		
Were their sentences a good length (20 words or less)?		
Did they use effective visuals?		
Was their voice pleasant and easy to understand?		
Did they use vocal variety?		
Did they pause well?		
Did their tone convey enthusiasm?		
Did they avoid the credibility killers—powerless language, filler words, and upspeak?		
Did they use gestures well?		
Did they smile?		
Did they have good eye contact?		
Were they relatable?		
Did they avoid jargon and legalese?		

About the Author

John Snow is a trial and appellate lawyer in Los Angeles. He has tried more than 30 cases to completion in state and federal court. He has tried civil and criminal cases, and he has represented plaintiffs and defendants. As a civil plaintiffs' lawyer, he has won multiple eight-figure trial awards for his clients.

John is currently the Director of Legal and Trial Training for the Los Angeles City Attorney's Office, one of the largest municipal law offices in the country, where he has trained hundreds of lawyers in trial advocacy, public speaking, and persuasion.

Before this role, John worked various stints in private practice and public service. He was a litigation partner at King, Holmes, Paterno, and Soriano, LLP, where he handled entertainment and intellectual property disputes for world-famous artists.

John also worked as a criminal prosecutor and civil enforcement lawyer litigating large public impact cases for the City of Los Angeles and People of the State of California. Before that, John was an associate at Hueston Hennigan LLP and Irell & Manella LLP, where he litigated complex business cases.

John started his career as a law clerk for the Honorable George H. King, former Chief Judge of the Central District of California. He has a JD from USC Gould School of Law and a BA in English Literature and Global Studies from the University of California, Santa Barbara. John also serves on the Board of Directors for Scribes, The American Society of Legal Writers.

Why I Wrote This Book

This book is a product of my quest to be a better speaker.

In my life, I have been bored to death by many presentations. Sometimes so much it made me angry because the speaker stole a moment of my life.

But I have also been deeply inspired by speakers. Some have moved me to action. The best ones have dramatically impacted me and showed me how to communicate in new and better ways.

For most of my career, I've been obsessed with learning to be the second kind of speaker and not the first.

It did not come naturally to me, so I watched many great (and not so great) lawyers in action. I jumped at every chance to get in the courtroom or present to a group. I tried different things. Sometimes I failed miserably. And I intensely studied the subject—reading and watching everything I could find.

When I started my quest, I saw that the speaking pedagogy for lawyers was not as developed as it should be. Nowhere near as much has been written about it compared to legal writing. So a thought formed in my mind that one day I might contribute something.

That day came when my main job became training other lawyers. It gave me time to think about speaking more intensely than I had before. And it gave me a unique window into what most people struggle with and how to improve it.

This book blends and condenses my years of research and experience—largely for me, but hopefully for others too.

I don't have the most experience in the subject, but I also don't have the least. I've learned that to teach someone something, you need to be only one step ahead of where they are. I hope this book finds people it can help.

Acknowledgments

Thank you to my parents. Without you this book would not be possible because without you, my life would not be possible. I have told you before that you did a good job, but now I get to do it in print. Thank you for giving me every opportunity you did, for supporting my education, and for giving me a safe and loving home. Dad, I miss you very much and wish you could read this. Mom, thank you for being the first person to read this and encouraging me along the way.

Thank you to Chelsea for being the best partner and sounding board. Your love, support, and approval helped me believe I had something to say. You gave me the confidence to do this. I am so lucky to be married to you.

Thank you to my grandmother for being the bravest person I know. Your selflessness and sacrifices—leaving war-torn Ukraine during WW2 for an unfamiliar country—made many happy lives possible, including mine.

Thank you to the rest of my family—my brothers, aunts, uncles, cousins, niece, nephew, and in-laws. All of you have supported me and for that I am very grateful.

Thank you to Jean Rosenbluth for being a wonderful friend and mentor for many years. You recognized my writing skills at a time I needed it and then made them so much better. I have learned so much from you.

Thank you to all my friends and colleagues from my professional life—from USC Law School to Judge King's chambers, from Irell & Manella and Hueston Hennigan to the Los Angeles City Attorney's Office, and to all the people at King, Holmes, Paterno and Soriano, LLP. Each of you shaped my growth as a lawyer. I believe this is ultimately a team sport. I'm lucky to have played it alongside many talented and kind people.

Thank you to all the trial attorneys responsible for the specific examples in this book, and those who gave quotes and tips. This book would not have been as good had I not been able to draw on your work in the courtroom.

Finally, thank you to the folks at Carolina Academic Press for believing in this book and making it happen.

Index